John Knox

by Wm. M. Taylor

PREFACE.

The sources from which the following narrative has been derived are (1) the splendidly edited and complete edition of Knox's Works in six volumes, by Dr. David Laing; (2) the Memoir of the Reformer, by Dr. Thomas McCrie, forming the first volume of the collected works of that eminent theologian; (3) the monograph by the late Professor Lorimer, D.D., entitled "John Knox and the Church of England"; and (4) the Histories of the Period, more especially that of Scotland, by John Hill Burton, vols. iii. and iv., and that of England, by J. A. Froude, vols. v. and vi. Some assistance also has been derived from "The Scottish Reformation," by Professor Lorimer; and the two sketches by Carlyle, the one in his "Heroes and Hero Worship," and the other in his essay on the Portraits {vi} of John Knox, have been both helpful and suggestive. Quotations have been generally indicated, but this acknowledgment must cover any accidental omission to give to each author his due; and for the rest the reader may be assured that while no material fact has been omitted, nothing has been recorded for which ample authority could not be given. The figure has been felt to be too large for the canvas to which we have been restricted, but we have sought to reproduce, as faithfully as possible the man as he was, and if we may succeed in removing any of the unreasonable prejudice, with which many still regard the Scottish Reformer, the story of his life will not be retold by us in vain.

W. M. T. NEW YORK.

CONTENTS.

CHAPTER I.

PAGE

CHAPTER III.

CHAPTER I.

EARLY LIFE AND CALL TO THE MINISTRY, 1505-1547.

On the sixteenth day of January, 1546, George Wishart delivered a remarkable sermon in the church of Haddington. Two things had combined to produce special depression in his heart. Shortly before he entered the pulpit a boy had put into his hands a letter informing him that his friends in Kyle would not be able to keep an appointment which they had made to meet him in Edinburgh. This news so saddened him that he expressed himself as "weary of the world," because he perceived that "men began to be weary of God." Nor was his despondency removed when he rose to preach, for instead of the crowds that used to assemble to hear him in that church, there were not more than a hundred persons present. It was thus made apparent to him that the efforts of his enemies for his overthrow were now to be successful, and so instead of treating the second table of the law as he had been expected to do, he poured forth a torrent of warning and denunciation, not unlike some of the fervid {2} utterances of the old Hebrew prophets. The effect produced was all the more solemn, because he evidently felt that he was bearing his last public testimony against the evils of his times.

When he had concluded he bade his friends farewell, and to John Knox, who throughout his sojourn in Lothian had attended him, armed with a two-handed sword, as a protection against the assassination with which he had twice been threatened, and who had pressed to be allowed to accompany him to Ormiston, where he was to spend the night, he said, "Nay, return to your bairns" (pupils), "and God bless you! One is sufficient for one sacrifice."

The good man's presentiment was all too surely realized. Before midnight the house in which he slept was surrounded by a band of which the Earl of Bothwell was the head, and he was given up by his host to that nobleman, only however on the receipt of a pledge, over which "hands" were "struck," to the effect that his personal safety should be secured, and he should not be delivered into his enemies' power. But promises in these days were not of much account, and Bothwell was easily prevailed upon to give him up to Cardinal Beaton, who took him first to Edinburgh Castle, and afterwards to St. Andrews. There, in defiance of the protest of the Regent, he was hurriedly subjected to the form of a trial by the cardinal, and being, of course, found guilty, he was executed at the stake on the first of March.

Thus it is, as the body-guard of Wishart, that we get our first glimpse of John Knox in history; and very characteristic of the man this first appearance was. He comes upon the scene as unheralded as Elijah, and, like him too, he is seen from the first to be set for the defence of the truth. He was a sword-bearer all through; only when he laid aside the two-handed brand which he carried before Wishart, he took in its stead "the sword of the Spirit, which is the word of God."

Before proceeding to tell the stirring story of his life, however, it may be well to take a brief survey of the condition of Scotland at the moment when he stepped into the arena of its national strife.

Little more than three years before the date of Wishart's execution, the Queen of Scotland had given birth to that Mary Stuart, whose character has been the puzzle of historians, and whose chequered career has been the theme of poets almost ever since. Her father, James V., broken-hearted by the utter defeat of his army by the English at the battle of Solway Moss, died only a few days after his daughter's birth. Thus it came about, that in a critical time which tested the statesmanship of the world's strongest rulers, alike in England, France, Germany, and Spain, Scotland had a baby sovereign, and the controlling of its affairs became an object of keen competition between contending parties. The queen-mother, Mary of Guise, a woman of marked ability, of much cunning, and of little principle, was, both from national and religious leanings, on {4} the side of the Catholic party. Of that party the head at this time was David Beaton, Archbishop of St. Andrews, and a Cardinal of the Church. This artful prelate, "the nephew of his uncle," was possessed of eminent talents, but was characterized by cruelty, licentiousness, and unscrupulousness. He had prevailed on James V. to violate the promise which he had made to his uncle, Henry VIII., to meet him at Newcastle. The haughty

Tudor had now broken with the Romish see, and was anxious, if possible, to induce his nephew to follow his example. But the cardinal, as great a master of intrigue as was the English king himself, had succeeded in keeping the Scottish monarch from putting himself under the spell of his uncle's influence, and Henry, exasperated at his defeat, sent into Scotland an army, whose success at Solway Moss led indirectly, as we have seen, to the death of James. When that event occurred, Beaton produced a forged will, purporting to be the last testament of the king, and nominating him as Regent with three of the nobles as his assistants. On the strength of that document he had himself proclaimed as Regent at the Cross of Edinburgh. But the validity of the instrument was annulled by the Scottish Parliament; and in the spring of 1543, James, Earl of Arran, heir presumptive of the crown, was appointed to the dignity which the cardinal had so eagerly, and so unrighteously sought to make his own.

This nobleman, "notorious," as Burton says, "for fickleness," had been at first on the side of the Reformation, {5} and was then assiduously courted by Henry VIII. He had even consented to the marriage of the baby queen to the young English Prince Edward. But the influence of the queen-mother and the cardinal, backed by that of his own natural brother, the Abbot of Paisley, together with the unjust and impolitic demands of the English monarch himself, combined to turn him from his original leanings. He publicly abjured the Protestant faith, and was received into the bosom of the Catholic Church. He broke off all negotiations for a matrimonial alliance between the royal houses of England and Scotland, and ultimately consented to the betrothal of Mary to the Dauphin of France. The result of these proceedings was a protracted war with England, during which Scotland was repeatedly invaded, and portions of it devastated by the southern forces.

But while these political and international intrigues, in which it must be confessed that there was little scrupulousness on either side, were going on, a great spiritual movement was making quiet progress among the people. The Reformation from Popery had begun in Scotland also. Patrick Hamilton, its protomartyr, had been put to death in 1528; but the smoke of his burning, to borrow the well-known words of one of the elder Beaton's own servants, "had infected all on whom it blew"; and the books of the German Reformers, together with the English Testaments of William Tyndale, had wrought like hidden leaven, especially among the more intelligent of the community. {6}

Thus we account for the fact that, in spite of legal prohibitions and public executions, the knowledge of evangelical truth was diffused, even when there was no living voice to proclaim it publicly in the hearing of the multitudes; so that when a man like Wishart did make his appearance, he found crowds to listen to him appreciatively both in Dundee and Ayr. The Lollards of Kyle had still worthy descendants in that historic district; and the merchants in towns like that of Leith, whose commerce brought them into contact with men from Hamburg, Antwerp, and the cities of the Rhine, were disposed to welcome the new doctrines. Among the nobles, men like Glencairn and Errol and Ruthven ranged themselves on the side of the Reformers; while the influence of a satirist like Sir David Lindsay of the Mount, and a scholar like Henry Balnaves of Halhill, was given heartily to their cause.

But next only to the diffusion of the Scriptures among the people, the greatest factor in the production of the Reformation in Scotland was the degraded condition into which in that country the Church of Rome itself had sunk. "That which decayeth is ready to vanish away." There were no longer in it the elements of vitality. It was past purifying, and had to be swept clean out. Its corruptions were too open to be denied, and too gross to be defended. The grasping selfishness and shameless licentiousness of the upper clergy were equalled only by the ignorance and general incompetence of the lower, so that there had sprung up among the people generally a {7} hatred of the order to which both belonged. This was deepened and intensified by the spirit in which the first efforts of the Reformers had been met, for in Scotland as elsewhere the prison and the stake were the short and easy answers made by papal intolerance to all the arguments which the preachers brought against the errors of Romanism. But these were answers which only turned more general attention to the statements of the Reformers, and gave wider circulation to their words. The storm of contrary wind unfurls the banner, and makes thereby its inscription the more legible, and in the same way the persecution of those who proclaimed the truth only fell out to the furtherance of that which it was designed to arrest.

But Cardinal Beaton's conscience was too hard to feel the crime, and his eye was too dim to see the blunder which he was committing in putting Wishart to death. He looked only at immediate results, and thought perhaps that by silencing the preacher he could arrest the influence of the words which had already gone from him. But in reality he was himself standing above a mine which before long exploded for his own destruction. His checkmating of Henry VIII. so exasperated that monarch that he entered into correspondence, through his agent Sir Robert Sadler, with certain Scotsmen whose disaffection to the cardinal was well known, and who, at his suggestion, or at least with his concurrence and approval, perhaps also with his reward, entered into a conspiracy to "take him out of the way." {8} Accordingly on the morning of the 29th of May, just three months after the martyrdom of Wishart, Cardinal Beaton was assassinated by a company of men headed by Norman Leslie. That the wily priest had himself been guilty of attempts to get rid of his adversaries by the same unscrupulous means is not to be denied. It is equally certain that, as things then were, it would have been impossible to bring him to trial for any of his enormities. But still the manner of his "taking off" is not only utterly indefensible, but also worthy of the deepest reprobation, and it is too true, as Dr. Lorimer has said, that "the exasperation of feeling called forth by a deed so daring and criminal gave rise to proceedings against the conspirators which, being extended to all their abettors real or supposed, had the effect of retarding the progress of the Reformation for many years, and of weighing it down with a load of opprobrium from the effects of which it could only slowly recover."[1]

Foreseeing that they would be the objects of bitter attack, the conspirators, after they had done their bloody work, resolved to keep possession of the Castle of St. Andrews which they had so unexpectedly seized, and there they were speedily joined by at least one hundred and forty persons, numbering among them Kirkaldy of Grange, Melville of Raith, Balfour of Mount-quhany, and many gentlemen of Fife and the neighbouring {9} counties. They put the castle into a state of defence, and were besieged by an army under command of the Regent Arran, against whom they held out, more perhaps from the incompetence of the besiegers than from the skill or strength of the besieged, until the end of January, 1547. At that date the siege was suspended under an agreement which stipulated that the Castle was still to remain in the hands of its defenders, on the conditions that they should hold it for the Regent and not deliver it to England; and that they should not be required to surrender it even to the Regent until he had obtained from Rome absolution for those who had been implicated in the murder of the cardinal. Upon his side the Regent agreed to withdraw his forces to the south of the Forth, and from the beginning of the year on till the following June the inmates of the Castle were permitted to go out and in at their pleasure, and to receive all that came to them.

Thus the Castle of St. Andrews became for the time a kind of sanctuary for all who were seeking relief or refuge from the oppression of the rulers in Church and State; and at the following Easter, which fell that year on the 10th of April, John Knox entered its gates under circumstances which he himself has thus described: "At the Pasch after, came to the Castle of St. Andrews John Knox, who, wearied of removing from place to place by reason of the persecution that came upon him by this Bishop of St. Andrews, was determined to have left Scotland and to have visited the schools of Germany {10} (of England then he had no pleasure by reason that the Pope's name being suppressed, his laws and corruptions remained in full vigour). But because he had the care of some gentlemen's children, whom certain years he had nourished in godliness, their fathers solicited him to go to St. Andrews, that himself might have the benefit of the castle, and their children the benefit of his doctrine, and so (we say) came he the time foresaid, to the said place, and having in his company Francis Douglas of Longniddry, George his brother, and Alexander Cockburn, eldest son to the laird of Ormiston, began to exercise them after his accustomed manner."[2]

Knox was at this time in the prime and vigour of his manhood, being forty-two years of age. He was born in 1505 at Gifford-gate, a suburb connected with Haddington by the old stone bridge across the Tyne. His parents were not distinguished either for rank or fortune, for one of his adversaries affirms that he was "obscuris natus parentibus" (born of obscure parents), and even one of his admirers says that "he descended but of lineage small." His father was William Knox, and his mother's name was Sinclair. Both of them apparently belonged to families that were in some way feudatories to the Earls of Bothwell, for at the Reformer's first interview with that earl, whose name is so tragically {11} coupled with Queen Mary's, he said, "Albeit that to this hour it hath not chanced me to speak to your lordship face to face, yet have I borne a good mind to your house; ... for, my lord, my grandfather, goodschir (i.e., according to Mr. Laing, maternal grandfather) and father have served your lordship's predecessors, and some of them have died under their standards." He received his earliest education at the Grammar School of Haddington, and passed when he was about sixteen years of age to the University of Glasgow, in the register of which his name appears among those of the students who were incorporated on the 25th October, 1522.

At that time and for a year later John Major, or Mair, Doctor of the Sorbonne, was Principal of the Glasgow University and Professor of Divinity in the same. He had some opinions, both ecclesiastical and political, which were considerably in advance of his age, and it has been supposed that Knox may have received from him some of those principles which he afterwards so ably advocated. But perhaps too much has been made of this by the Reformer's biographers, for Major remained only one year in Glasgow after Knox had been registered as a student at the University; and though he held some liberal notions in politics, he was in theology to the last a rigid scholastic. Moreover, he was so far from being a zealous promoter of the cause of the Reformation that his name appears as a judge on several of the tribunals at which the early Scottish {12} confessors were condemned to banishment or death. Taking these things into consideration along with the youth of Knox when he first entered college, it will appear hardly likely that he received from Major anything more than a general impulse in the direction of liberty and liberality, which prepared him to look with favour on the efforts of those who, though they might be called innovators, were in reality only seeking to get back to the original simplicity of the gospel, and the primitive purity of the Church.

Knox left Glasgow without taking the degree of Master of Arts, and there is no evidence whatever for the statement sometimes made that he was afterwards connected with the University of St. Andrews. In fact we lose sight of him entirely for a period of eighteen years from the time of his leaving Glasgow. During that interval he was ordained a priest, though by whom, or at what precise date, it is now impossible to determine; but his signature has been found,[3] as notary, to an instrument in the charter-room at Tyninghame, bearing date March 27, 1543, a fact which establishes that up till that time he retained his character as a priest and had the papal authority to act as a notary. With these functions he seems to have combined that of a teacher of youth, for at the time we come upon him in connection with Wishart, he had under his charge some young men of good family in the land.

We have no details concerning his conversion from the Romish to the Protestant faith. According to one authority it was Thomas Guillaume who was "the first to give Mr. Knox a taste of the truth." That eloquent preacher,-- a native of East Lothian, who had risen to a high place in the order of the

Dominicans,--had through the influence of the party of progress been appointed chaplain to the Regent Arran at the time when that weak ruler was favouring the Reformers. Knox himself has described him as "a man of solid judgment, reasonable letters (as for that age), and of prompt and good utterance; his doctrine was wholesome without great vehemency against superstition." It does not appear, however, from anything he says that he ever came personally into contact with him, though it is possible that some of those clear expositions of Scripture for which Guillaume was so esteemed may have been heard by him, and may have produced a deep impression on his mind. But beyond all question George Wishart was the true spiritual father of John Knox. The preaching and companionship of that earnest man during that journey through the Lothians, which ended in his apprehension at Ormiston, did more for Knox than any other human instrumentality whatever. They wrought conviction in him, and brought him out into decision, so that from the moment when these two men parted from each other for the last time at the church of Haddington, it was no longer possible for Knox to return into the position of comparative obscurity from which he had {14} emerged to become the body-guard of Wishart. He had come prominently out on the side of the Reformation, and the martyrdom of his teacher would only deepen his determination that he should not go back.

But there was no need for him to throw his life away as a gratuitous sacrifice, and therefore, when he was compelled to seek safety from his persecutors by removing from place to place, and out of weariness was minded to go to Germany, he consented, at the earnest solicitations of the parents of his pupils, to find protection in the Castle of St. Andrews. Let it be noted, however, that he did not enter that stronghold until the 10th of April, 1547, that is, more than ten months after Beaton's murder, and therefore he is not to be reckoned among those who had concocted and carried out the assassination of that prelate. He was at that date in too obscure a station to be in any way, even the most remote, associated with those who had committed that foul murder, and he went to St. Andrews simply that he might be able to carry on uninterruptedly the education of his pupils. Accordingly, so soon as he was fairly settled there, he resumed the regular routine of his work with them. What that was he has himself informed us in these words: "Besides their grammar and other humane authors" (that is, authors in what were then called the humanity classes) "he read unto them a catechism, an account whereof he caused them to give publicly in the parish church of St. Andrews. He read moreover unto them the Gospel of John proceeding where he" (had) {15} "left" (off) "at his departing from Longniddry where before his residence was, and that lecture he read in the chapel within the castle at a certain hour." These public exercises attracted to them a large number of those who were then sojourning in the castle, among whom were Henry Balnaves of Halhill, a distinguished jurist, who had been already, and was to be again, one of the judges of the court of session, and John Rough, who was the stated preacher to the congregation within the castle. These men were greatly impressed alike with the matter, the method, and the manner of delivery of the lectures, and seeing his fitness for the work, they earnestly entreated Knox to enter at once upon the office of the ministry. But he declared that "he would not run where God had not called him," and peremptorily refused to accede to their request. Upon this they took counsel with Sir David Lindsay, of the Mount, and others, and ultimately agreed that Rough, without giving any formal warning that he was about to do anything of the kind, should address to Knox a special public call in the name and before the face of the congregation. Accordingly, in the presence of the people, and after having preached a sermon on the election of ministers, Rough turned to Knox and said, "Brother, ye shall not be offended, albeit that I speak unto you that which I have in charge even from all those that are here present, which is this: In the name of God and of His Son Jesus Christ, and in the name of these that presently call you by my mouth, I charge you that ye refuse {16} not this holy vocation, but that, as ye tender the glory of God, the increase of Christ's kingdom, the edification of your brethren, and the comfort of me whom you understand well enough to be oppressed by the multitude of labours, that ye take upon you the public office and charge of preaching even as ye look to avoid God's heavy displeasure, and desire that He shall multiply His graces with you." Then turning to the congregation he said, "Was not this your charge to me?" They answered, "It was, and we approve it." The combined suddenness and solemnity of this appeal completely unmanned Knox. He burst into tears and hastened to his closet, where we may well believe that he sought light from God; and the result Was that he was led to take up that ministry which he laid down only with his life. Not from the impulse of caprice, or because he desired the position of a preacher, but because he could not otherwise meet the responsibility which God had laid upon him, did he enter upon that high and honourable vocation. He was to do a work for his countrymen not unlike that which Moses did for his kinsmen, and so like Moses he was called to it in the full maturity of his powers, and entered upon it with the conviction that God had given him his commission, and he dared not disobey.

Nor did he tarry long before he began to preach, for the call of Providence came almost simultaneously with that of the church. It happened just then that Mr. Rough was engaged in a controversy with a popish {17} dean named Annand. For such a discussion Rough was but poorly furnished, since, as McCrie says, though he was sound in doctrine, his literary acquirements were only moderate. In his emergency he had been much assisted by Knox, who made such good use of the pen that he beat back his adversary from all his defences. As a last resort Annand took refuge in the authority of the Church, upon which Knox at once exclaimed, in the hearing of those who were present at the discussion, that a distinction must be drawn between the true spouse of Christ and the Church of Rome, and offered to prove by word or writing that the Papal Church had degenerated from that of primitive times more than the Jews who crucified the Saviour had fallen from the ordinances of Moses. On hearing this, the people alleged that they could not all read his writings, but could all listen to his preaching, and therefore insisted, in the name of God, that he would let them hear his proof of the assertion which he had made. Such an appeal was not to be resisted, and therefore on the very next Sunday Knox entered the pulpit, and preached (from the text Daniel vii. 24, 25) a sermon, in which, after having given the true marks of the Church, he went on to expose the corruptions of the Romish clergy in their lives, the erroneous doctrine taught by them, especially in the matter of justification, and the enslaving laws enjoined by them in regard to days, and meats, and marriage. In particular he inveighed against the blasphemies of popery. He identified the Papal {18} Church with the Babylonian harlot in the book of the Revelation, and concluded by demanding the most thorough investigation of all the statements which he had made, and the most minute examination of the authorities whom he had cited. This discourse was listened to by a large assembly, among whom was John Major, his old Glasgow principal, and it produced a great effect upon all. Some said, "Others lopped off the branches of the papistry, but he strikes at the root to destroy the whole." Others predicted that he would meet the fate of Wishart, who had never spoken quite so plainly as Knox had done that day. The new archbishop of St. Andrews, not yet consecrated to his office, expostulated with the vicar-general of the diocese for allowing such heretical doctrines to be promulgated without opposition, and that led to the calling of a convention of the learned men of the abbey and the university, before which Rough and Knox were summoned to make answer to nine articles, involving heresies, which had been drawn from their sermons. But nothing more serious resulted from that meeting than a debate between Knox and a friar named Arbuckle, whose arguments Knox easily refuted, and that too with a considerable mixture of the grim humour which ever and anon laughs outright in the pages of his history. Clearly, therefore, it would be a perilous thing for the Church to let such a man do all the preaching to the people; and so orders were issued that each of the learned men in the abbey and university should preach {19} in his own turn on the Sundays in the parish church. This deprived Knox of the opportunity of addressing the congregation on those days when the greatest numbers were in attendance; but he continued his ministry on the other days of the week, and that with such success that although it lasted in all at this time not more than three months, many of the inhabitants of the town renounced popery, and made confession of the Protestant faith by partaking of the Lord's Supper in the reformed manner, the first occasion on which the ordinance was publicly administered in Scotland after that fashion.

Thus the beginning of Knox's work marks a distinct stage in the history of the Scottish Reformation. At first, and under what has been called by Lorimer the Hamilton period, peculiar emphasis was laid upon the truths which were revived in the teaching of Luther; under the Wishart period the doctrine of the sacraments came into prominence, and then first the influence of Switzerland began to be felt by Scotland; but under Knox attention was directed especially to the nature and constitution of the church, and the first sermon which he preached, and of which we have given the barest outline, had already in it "the promise and the potency" of the great work which he was yet to accomplish for his native land.

[1] "The Scottish Reformation." A Historical Sketch by Peter Lorimer, D.D. London: R. Griffin & Co., 1860, p. 157.

[2] "The Works of John Knox," collected and edited by Dr. David Laing, vol. i. p. 185. Once for all let it be said that in making these quotations the spelling is modernized, but otherwise no alteration is made.

[3] By Dr. David Laing: see "Knox's Works," vol. vi. pp. xxii. xxiii.

CHAPTER II.

IN THE FRENCH GALLEYS, 1547-1549.

During the months which had elapsed since the time when the Castle of St. Andrews had become a refuge for those who had so summarily and unscrupulously murdered Beaton, changes had occurred both in England and in France which deeply affected their interests. Henry VIII. died on the 28th January, 1547, and for a short time during the minority of Edward the reins of government had been virtually given into the hands of the Duke of Somerset, under the name of Protector. This deprived the besieged of their most powerful friend, for although after Henry's decease the Privy Council fulfilled his directions and voted money to Leslie and others as individuals, together with a certain sum for the maintenance of a garrison in the castle, yet Somerset took little further care of those who remained within its shelter, and left them virtually to their own resources. The death of Francis I. of France, which took place on the 31st of March in the same year, added to their danger, for he was succeeded by Henry II., who as Dauphin had been the leader of the party {21} most opposed to England, and who was therefore by no means indisposed to do anything that would tend to widen the breach between that country and his own. When therefore Somerset, unwisely insisting on reviving the pretensions of feudal superiority over Scotland which had been put forth by Edward I., permitted the Borders to be wasted by fire and sword, and urged the French to abstain from interference, he was met with the reply that their king "might not suffer the old friends of France to be oppressed and alienated from him." In France, therefore, the Regent Arran and the queen-mother found a willing ally, and in the beginning of June Leo Strozzi, prior of Capua, appeared with a fleet of French galleys in sight of the Castle of St. Andrews, and demanded the surrender of its inmates. According to agreement this was conditioned on the reception from Rome of absolution for the murderers of Beaton. But although Strozzi brought absolution with him, it was expressed in such an equivocal form,--"Remittimus irremissibile," we pardon that which is unpardonable,--that the persons interested refused to accept it, and the siege was renewed. Arran, hearing of the arrival of his allies, hastened from the west country to co-operate with them, and the result was such as might have been expected. For this time the defenders had to contend with skilled gunners, before whose batteries, as Knox had forewarned them would be the case, "their walls were no better than eggshells." From the steeple of St. Salvador's College and the towers of the Abbey, as well as from the galleys in {22} the bay, the cannon of their assailants poured shot in upon them, while within the walls the plague broke out with virulence. So in the end of July Kirkcaldy of Grange went forth with a flag of truce to make the best possible terms with the victors. The conditions obtained were that the lives of all within the castle, whether English or Scotch, should be spared; that they should be safely transported to France; and that in case, upon conditions that by the king of France should be offered unto them, they could not be content to remain in service and freedom there, they should, at the expense of the king of France, be safely conveyed to what country they would require, other than Scotland. These promises, however, were shamefully broken, for the vanquished were taken on board the vessels which had been plentifully loaded with the spoils of the castle, and carried to France, where they were held in bondage for many months. One detachment of them was taken to Cherbourg, and another to Mount St. Michael. Knox himself was reduced to the condition of a galley-slave.

We have no connected account of his experiences in this time of trial, but here and there in his works he has dropped incidental hints which give us glimpses of his sufferings, and of the manner in which they were endured by him. In his history of the Reformation, in connection with the account of an effort made by some of his friends to dissuade him in the year 1559 from preaching in St. Andrews, we have a report of the answer which he gave to them, and in that occurs the following passage: {23} "In this town and church began God first to call me to the dignity of a preacher, from, the which I was reft by the tyranny of France by procurement of the bishops as ye all well enough know. How long I continued prisoner, what torment I sustained in the galleys, and what were the sobs of my heart, is now no time to consider." An equally pathetic reference to his misery during this season of bondage, and to his solace under it, is to be found in his treatise on the true nature and object of prayer, in which after having referred to the words, (Ps. vii. 16, 17) "His mischief shall return upon his own head, and his violent dealings shall come down upon his own pate. I will praise the Lord according to His righteousness, and will sing praise to the name of the Lord most high," he goes on to say, "This is not written for David only, but for all such as shall suffer tribulation to the end of the world. For I, the writer hereof (let this be said to the laud and praise of God alone), in anguish of mind and vehement tribulation and affliction, called to the Lord, when not only the ungodly, but even my faithful brethren, yea and mine own self, that is all natural understanding in me, judged my cause to be irremediable; and yet in my greatest calamity, and when my pains were most cruel, would His eternal wisdom that I should write far contrary to the judgment of carnal wisdom, which His mercy has proved true. Blessed be His holy name! And therefore I dare be bold, in the verity of God's word to promise that notwithstanding the vehemence of trouble, the long continuance thereof, the {24} dispersion of all men, the fearfulness, danger, dolor, and anguish of our hearts; yet if we call constantly to God, that beyond expectation of all men, He shall deliver." There can be little doubt, as Dr. Laing remarks in a foot-note to this passage, that Knox here refers to his bodily and mental sufferings during his confinement on board the French galley, and so we see that his faith was not a mere sentimental thing, that, as he has himself elsewhere expressed it, he was no mere "speculative theologue," but indeed a steadfast believer, who had proved God's faithfulness to His promise even in the sorest tribulation.

Again in the epistle to the congregation of the Castle of St. Andrews prefixed by him to the tract on Justification by Faith, which his friend Henry Balnaves had written during his imprisonment at Rouen, we find among other allusions to his support under his sufferings the following words: "I exhort that ye read diligently this treatise, not only with earnest prayer that ye may understand the same aright, but also with humble and due thanksgiving unto our most merciful Father, who of His infinite power hath so strengthened the hearts of His prisoners, that in despite of Satan they desist not yet to work, but in the most vehemency of tribulation seek the utility and salvation of others."

And in a letter written in December, 1559, he speaks of "all the torments of the galleys" in such a way as to lead us to conclude that he was subjected to the greatest hardships. Once more, and perhaps most pathetically of {25} all, in that letter to the congregation of Berwick which Dr. Lorimer first printed in his "John Knox and the Church of England," and to which we shall have to make fuller reference by-and-by, he thus writes: "This day I am more vile and of low reputation in my own eyes than I was either that day that my feet were chained in the prison of dolor (the galleys I mean), or yet that day that I was delivered by His only providence from the same."

It is clear, therefore, that his sufferings were severe, and while he endured them with a fortitude that was sustained by his faith in God, he was careful also to maintain always a conscience void of offence. He tells us that those who were in the galleys "were threatened with torments if they would not give reverence to the mass, but they could never make the poorest of that company to give reverence to that idol." He adds the following narrative, and from the ironic humour that plays about his style as he recites it, we cannot doubt that he was himself the hero of the story. "Soon after the arrival at Nantes, their great salve was sung, and a glorious (gaudy) painted board was brought in to be kissed, and amongst others was presented to one of the Scotchmen then chained. He gently said, 'Trouble me not; such an idol is accursed, and therefore I will not touch it.' The patron and the arguesyn (i.e. sergeant who commanded) with two officers, having the chief charge of all such matters, said, 'Thou shalt handle it,' and so they violently thrust it to his face, and put it betwixt his hands, who seeing the extremity, taking the {26} idol, and advisedly looking about, he cast it into the river, and said, 'Let our lady now save herself; she is light enough; let her learn to swim.' After that was no Scotchman urged with that idolatry."

But sorely bestead as he was in his captivity, he would not sanction any attempt to escape which should savour of violence. Though himself innocent of all complicity in Beaton's murder, he had seen the cause which he had at heart so greatly hindered by the consequences of that evil deed, and he was withal so utterly opposed to everything which he believed that God had forbidden, that he would be no party to doing evil that good might come. Accordingly when Kirkcaldy and two other friends who were confined with him at Mount St. Michael wrote to him to inquire whether they might with safe conscience break their prison, he replied, that if without the shedding of any blood they could set themselves at liberty, they might do so without sin, but that he would never consent to their slaying of others in order to obtain deliverance. He added the expression of his own assurance that God Himself would work out their enlargement in such a way that "the praise thereof should redound to His glory alone." Nor was that with him a mere temporary or intermittent sentiment. It was the settled conviction of his soul; for from the very beginning of his captivity when one of his fellow-prisoners would often ask him if he thought that they should ever be delivered, his invariable answer was that "God would deliver them from that bondage {27} to His glory, even in this life." Nor did he falter, even when his own strength seemed ebbing out, for when the galleys had returned to Scotland in the summer of

1548, and were lying between Dundee and St. Andrews, while he himself was so reduced by illness that his life was despaired of, the same companion bidding him look to the land, asked him if he knew it, whereupon he made reply, "Yes, I know it well, for I see the steeple of that place where God first opened my mouth to His glory, and I am fully persuaded, how weak soever I now appear, that I shall not depart this life till that my tongue shall glorify His holy name in the same place." He tells this almost as if he believed that the Spirit of prophecy spoke through him at the moment; but it is not necessary for us, while admitting the full truth of the narrative, to accept any such explanation. If his anticipation had not been verified, his words might have been entirely forgotten; and the probability is that his conviction rested rather upon his general apprehension of the principles of the Divine administration, than upon any supernatural communication of a special sort. The Psalmist writes that "the secret of the Lord is with them that fear Him;" and this gracious illumination, which is the heritage of all in the proportion in which they possess the character with which it is associated, is sufficient to account for the correctness of his impression, without having recourse to the theory of prophetic inspiration. That even Knox himself would have thus regarded this matter, seems clear from a passage in {28} his "Faithful Admonition to the Professors of God's Truth in England," which Dr. Lorimer thinks is of standard authority as giving the principle of interpretation for all those places in which he speaks in what may be called a prophetic tone and manner; and in which it has sometimes been thought that he spoke not without some endowment of supernatural insight and foreknowledge. We quote the following sentences: "But ye would know the grounds of my certitude. God grant that hearing them, ye may understand and steadfastly believe the same. My assurances are not marvels of Merlin, nor yet the dark sentences of profane prophecies; but (1) the plain truth of God's word, (2) the invincible justice of the everlasting God, and (3) the ordinary course of His punishments and plagues from the beginning, are my assurances and grounds" (p. 85).

But however we may account for the assurance which he felt, his forecast of the future was certainly remarkably fulfilled; and there are few contrasts in history more striking and suggestive than that between the weak and apparently dying galley-slave looking longingly on the shores of his native land; and the energetic Reformer of a later date, of whom the English ambassador wrote to Cecil saying: "I assure you the voice of one man is able in an hour to put more life in us than six hundred trumpets continually blustering in our ears."

CHAPTER III.

MINISTRY IN BERWICK-ON-TWEED, 1549-1550.

By what means Knox obtained his release from the galling servitude in which he had been held by the French, we have not been able to discover; but it is believed that he was indebted for it to the intercession of England, and it is certain that in the early part of the year 1549, he was employed by the Privy Council of that country as one of the ministers whom its members commissioned to preach the doctrines of the Reformation throughout the kingdom. The probability is that he arrived in London about the month of February, and it is conjectured that as Henry Balnaves was in that city as a commissioner from the besieged in St. Andrews, at the time of the death of Henry VIII., Knox, who had just then entered upon his ministry, may have been beholden to his friend for bringing his name to the favourable notice of the English Reformers. But however that may have been, we come upon authentic and reliable information, when we find in the register of the Privy Council, under date April 7th, 1549, an entry authorizing the payment of five pounds "to {30} John Knox, preacher, by way of reward." Besides this, his name occurs as the sixty-fourth in a list of eighty who obtained licence to preach in England during the reign of Edward the Sixth. He himself informs us in his History, that "he was first appointed preacher to Berwick, then to Newcastle; last he was called to London and to the southern parts of England, where he remained till the death of Edward the Sixth." This is all that he has said directly in that work concerning his residence in England; but so much new light has been shed on this part of the Reformer's career by the painstaking and elaborate monogram of Dr. Lorimer, that we are now able to follow his steps with something like minuteness.

He was settled first at the border town of Berwick-on-Tweed, which in those days was "the focus of a long and bloody war between the two kingdoms, which had begun with the tremendous slaughter of the Scots at Pinkey in the autumn of 1547, and in which the Scots, having received large assistance from France, were still able to maintain so vigorous a defence that there was no near prospect of a return of peace."[1] Thus it happened that its garrison was larger than ordinary, and everything about the place was volcanic. Quarrels among the soldiers were common, and the civilians themselves were not over peaceful, so that the chronic state of the town was one of disorder. John Brende, "master of the musters," reports to the Protector Somerset concerning {31} it: "There is better order among the Tartars than in this town; the whole picture of the place is one of social disorder and the worst police."[2] Besides all this, the great majority of the people were as yet probably papists, for the doctrines of the Reformation had made little progress thus far in the northern counties, and matters ecclesiastical were very unsettled. In March of that year the first Prayer-Book of Edward VI. was sanctioned by Parliament and published for the use of the Church. The new liturgy still retained much of the leaven of sacerdotalism and sacramentarianism, but it was decidedly in advance of anything which could have been issued in the days of Henry VIII. It was thoroughly approved by but a portion of the bishops, and there were several counties in the remoter parts of the kingdom where it was never introduced at all. Tunstall, then Bishop of Durham, who was no friend to the cause of reform, was in no haste to give effect to the new legislation; and the council of the north, to which was committed the care of public affairs in that then distant corner of the realm, probably thought it advisable to refrain from enforcing it upon the people, until they were prepared, by the instructions of some eminent preacher, for receiving and obeying it. Thus we account for the fact that, all the time he was in Berwick, Knox was left very much to his own discretion as to the doctrines which he preached, and the methods {32} which he adopted for the conduct of Divine service and the administration of the sacraments.

Already in his preface to Balnaves's treatise on Justification, the first of his printed productions so far as can be traced, he had written a summary of his belief on that great central doctrine; and in his disputation with Arbuckle in St. Andrews, he had been truly charged with holding the following opinions--viz. first, man may neither make nor devise a religion that is acceptable to God, but is bound to observe and keep the religion that from God is received without chopping or changing thereof; second, the sacraments of the New Testament ought to be ministered as they were instituted by Christ Jesus and practised by the apostles, nothing ought to be added to them, nothing ought to be diminished from them; third, the mass is abominable idolatry, blasphemous to the death of Christ, and a profanation of the Lord's Supper. When therefore he began his labours at Berwick he set himself to the proclamation of the great truths which radiate from the priesthood of Christ; and in his dispensation of the supper he followed an order of his own, which was not improbably the same as he had adopted in the Castle of St. Andrews. This is put beyond dispute by his letter to the congregation of Berwick, written probably about the close of 1552, and the fragment entitled "The Practice of the Lord's Supper used in Berwick-upon-Tweed by John Knox, preacher to the congregation of the Church there," both of which are to be found in {33} Dr. Lorimer's Appendix. The matter is of more than mere antiquarian interest, and we may therefore make one or two extracts from the more important of these documents.

In regard to his preaching he thus writes: "As for the variety and diversity of opinions touching the doctrine and chief points of religion which ye have received, God I take to witness, and the Lord Jesus Christ, before whom at once shall all flesh appear, that I never taught unto you, nor unto any others my auditory, that doctrine as necessary to be believed which I did not find written in God's holy law and testament. And, therefore, in that case with Paul I will say, 'If an angel from heaven shall teach unto you another gospel than ye have heard and externally received, let him be accursed.'" Then after stating in a positive form what he understands by the gospel he adds: "If in any of these chief and principal points any man vary from that doctrine which ye have professed, let him be accursed:[3] (1) as if any man teach any other cause moving God to elect and choose us than His own infinite goodness and mere mercy; (2) any other name in heaven or under the heaven wherein salvation stands, but only the name of Jesus; (3) any other means whereby we are justified and absolved from wrath and damnation that our sins deserve, than by faith only; (4) any other cause or end of good works than that first we are made good trees, and thereafter bring {34} forth fruits accordingly, to witness that we are lively members of Christ's holy and most sanctified body, prepared vessels to the honour and praise of our Father's glory; (5) if any teach prayers to be made to other than God above; (6) if any Mediator betwixt God and man, but only our Lord Jesus; (7) if more or other sacraments be affirmed or required to be used than Christ Jesus left ordinary in His Church, to wit, Baptism and the Lord's Table, or mystical supper; (8) if any deny remission of sins, resurrection of the flesh and life everlasting to appertain to us in Christ's blood, which, sprinkled in our hearts by faith, doth purge us from all sin; so that we need no more nor other sacrifices than that oblation once offered for all, by the which God's elect be fully sanctified and made perfect; if any I say, require any other sacrifice to be made for sins than Christ's death, which once He suffered, or any other manner whereby Christ's death may be applied to man, than by faith only, which also is the gift of God, so that man hath no cause to glory in works; and yet, if any deny good works to be profitable as not necessary to a true Christian profession, let the affirmers, teachers, or maintainers of such a doctrine be accursed of you, as they are of God unless they repent." In these articles we are struck with the absence of all reference to the Holy Spirit and regeneration; but we have many allusions to these subjects elsewhere, some, indeed, in this very document, and we may suppose that as it was specifically the mediatorial work of Christ that was then in controversy, {35} he designedly restricted himself to that. But from this summary, brief as it is, we learn that even at this early date, long before he had visited Geneva, or met Calvin, Knox had found his own way by the study of the Scriptures to those views of gospel truth which are now associated with the name of the great Frenchman; and that they formed the chief themes of his public discourse at Berwick is evident from the solemn words with which he has here introduced their enumeration.

Nor was his proclamation of them there in vain; for in his vindication of himself, at a later date before Queen Mary of Scotland, from the charge of causing great sedition and slaughter in England, and securing his ends by necromancy, he said among other things, "I shame not further to affirm that God so blessed my weak labours, that in Berwick, where commonly before there used to be slaughter by reason of quarrels that used to arise among the soldiers, there was as great quietness all the time that I remained there, as there is this day in Edinburgh."[4] Besides this, there is in the letter from which we have quoted abundant evidence that his biographer was not wrong when he affirmed that during his two years in Berwick numbers were converted and a visible reformation was produced upon the soldiers of the garrison who had been notorious for turbulence and licentiousness.

But his procedure in regard to the Lord's Supper was even more remarkable for its independence, than {36} the tenour of his discourses was for its adherence to the Pauline theology. In the Book of Common Prayer issued by the joint authorization of Convocation and Parliament in 1549, the rubric for the Lord's Supper provided that bread "unleavened and round as it was afore" should be used. But in regard to that Knox took the bold course of ignoring the authoritative rubrics. He substituted common bread for the wafer, and he administered the "elements" to the people while they sat, according to the form still followed in the nonconforming churches of England, and the Presbyterian churches in all parts of the world. It may seem to some that this was a defiance of the law; and perhaps in strictest construction so it was; but it is to be remembered that, as yet, the law had not become operative in the district to which Berwick belonged, and that therefore it was open meanwhile for Knox to take the course which he believed to be best. Thus he writes:[5] "Kneeling at the Lord's Supper I have proved by doctrine (teaching) to be no convenient gesture for a table; (a gesture) which hath been given in that action to such a presence of Christ, as no place of God's Scripture doth teach unto us. And therefore, kneeling in that action, appearing to be joined with certain dangers, no less in maintaining superstition than in using Christ's holy institution with other gestures than either He used or commanded to be used, I thought good amongst you to avoid and to {37} use sitting at the Lord's Table; which ye did not refuse, but with all reverence and thanksgiving to God for His truth knowing, as I suppose, ye confirmed the doctrine with your gestures and confession." The order which he observed[6] began with a sermon on the benefits given us by God through Jesus Christ; this was followed by prayer, after which was read the account of the institution of the ordinance from 1 Corinthians xi. 20-30. Then a declaration of "what persons be unworthy to be partakers" was made; after which "common prayer was offered in the form of confession." At the conclusion of this prayer, some notable passage in which God's mercy is most evidently declared was read from the gospel, and thereafter the minister pronounced absolution to such as unfeignedly repent and believe in Jesus Christ. After this came prayer for the congregation and for the sovereign.

At this point the fragment which we have been following breaks off, but there is every reason to believe that the remainder of the service was the same as that afterwards adopted in Scotland; and any one at all conversant with the ecclesiastical ritual of the Presbyterian churches in that country may see in the portion which we have given the origin of the "action" sermon, the "fencing of the tables;" and the frequent if not invariable use of the passage from first Corinthians as the "warrant" for the observance of the Supper, {38} which characterize a communion "occasion" in that country. But the singular thing about the matter is that this Puritan and Presbyterian form of administering the ordinance of the Lord's Supper was observed in England by John Knox when he was labouring at Berwick as a recognised minister of the Church of England, and acting under the authority, or perhaps, to put it more correctly, with the permission, of the government. This was at a date anterior by ten years to the time when it was introduced into Scotland with the sanction of its Parliament.

But it deserves notice that although Knox was thus conscientiously opposed to kneeling at the Lord's Table, he was not so intolerant as to declare that the taking of that posture at that table was necessarily sinful. The reader of the letter addressed to the congregation at Berwick cannot fail to be struck with the broad Pauline spirit manifested by the Reformer in his treatment of this subject. He is advising his friends as to what they should do if, now that he had ceased to have the oversight of them, the practice of kneeling at the communion table should be insisted upon; and he affirms that he neither recants nor repents his former teaching, but still prefers sitting to any other posture; yet he adds[7] "because I am but one having in my contrair, magistrates, common order, and judgments of many learned, I am not minded for maintenance of that one thing to gainstand the magistrates in all and {39} other chief points of religion agreeing with Christ, and His true doctrine, nor yet to break nor trouble common Order, thought meet to be kept for unity and peace in the congregations for a time. And least of all do I intend to condemn or lightly regard the grave judgments of such men as unfeignedly I fear (reverence), love and will obey, in all things judged expedient to promote God's glory, these subsequents granted to me." Then follow three conditions which may be summarized thus,--first, that the magistrates make known that kneeling is not required for any superstitious reasons or for any adoration of Christ's natural body believed to be there present, but only for the sake of uniform Order and that for a time; second, that kneeling is not imposed as a thing essential to the right observance of the ordinance, or required by Christ, but enjoined only as a ceremony thought seemly by men; and third, that the brethren shall have regard to his conscience, and not bring any uncharitable accusation against him, because he seeks to follow what Christ has commanded rather than what men have required. With these concessions granted, he declares that he would be satisfied; and that there may be no breach of charity, he recommends his former flock, should these conditions be complied with, to conform to the requirements of the Prayer-Book if those in authority should insist on their so doing. We have been the more particular in bringing out this fact at this particular time, because of its bearing on his conduct in connection with the {40} issue of the revised Prayer-Book in 1552, of which we shall have to speak more particularly by-and-by.

So much for the Reformer's public work in Berwick; but before we accompany him to Newcastle, we must pause to mention that it was during his residence at this time in the border town that he made the acquaintance of and was engaged to the lady who afterwards became his wife. Her name was Marjory Bowes, and she was the daughter of Richard Bowes, youngest son of Sir Ralph Bowes, of Streatham. Her mother was Elizabeth, daughter of Sir Robert Aske, of Aske. The father, probably on account of Knox's religious opinions, was opposed to the marriage, and so the union was deferred for some years. But the mother was friendly to the Reformer, and with her he kept up a constant correspondence in which many of the softer traits of his character come beautifully out. Mrs. Bowes was subject to religious melancholy, and the tender manner in which he often seeks in his letters to bind up her bruised spirit shows that, when occasion needed, he could be a "son of consolation" as well as a "son of thunder." Sometimes too, as when his heart was stirred with solicitude for the spiritual interests of those among whom he had laboured, or when he was required to confront the possible issue of his uncompromising adherence to what he believed to be right, he rises to a strain of heroism which reminds us of the greatest of the apostles. One example of this occurs in his letter to his Berwick friends, and we may fitly {41} close this chapter by reproducing it here. "If any man be offended with me that I, willing to avoid God's wrath and vengeance threatened against such as having no necessity despise His ordinances, do purpose and intend to obey God, embracing such as He has offered unto me (rather) than to please and flatter man that unjustly held the same from me; if any, I say, for this cause be offended and will seek my displeasure or trouble, let the same understand, that as I have a body, which only they may hurt, and not unless God so permit; so have they bodies and souls which both shall God punish in fire inextinguishably with the devil and his angels, unless suddenly they repent and cease to malign against God and His holy ordinance. With life and death, dear brethren, I am at point,--they before me in equal balances. Transitory life is not so sweet to me that for defence thereof I will jeopard to lose the life everlasting. Nor yet is corporeal death to me so fearful that albeit most certainly I understood the same shortly to follow my godly purpose, I would therefore depone myself to die in God's wrath and anger for ever and ever, which no doubt I should do, if for man's pleasure I refused God's perfect ordinance."[8] There is no mistaking the ring of such words as these; and lie who wrote them takes his place in the honourable company of the heroes of conscience to whom the world no less than the Church has owed so much.

[1] Lorimer, p. 17.

[2] Lorimer, p. 18

[3] Lorimer, pp. 257-8.

[4] Lorimer, p. 16.

[5] Lorimer, p. 261.

[6] Lorimer, p. 290.

[7] Lorimer, pp. 261-2.

[8] Lorimer, p. 260.

CHAPTER IV.

KNOX AND THE ENGLISH BOOK OF COMMON PRAYER, 1551-1553.

From Berwick Knox was removed, in the early summer of 1551, to Newcastle-on-Tyne, where he laboured, with occasional absences, for nearly two years. Already, in the spring of 1550, he had made a public discourse of great importance there, and perhaps the impression produced by his words then, may have led to his being ultimately transferred thither. There is extant among his writings "A Vindication of the Doctrine that the Sacrifice of the Mass is Idolatry," to which this note is prefixed: "The fourth of April, in the year 1550, was appointed to John Knox, preacher of the Holy Evangel of Jesus Christ, to give his confession why he affirmed the mass idolatry; which day, in presence of the Council, and congregation, amongst whom was also present the Bishop of Durham, in this manner he beginneth." This has been supposed by some to indicate that he was under accusation of heresy, and had been called to Newcastle to make his defence. But though it is not unlikely that his {43} doctrine had been objected to by Tunstall, yet the Council of the North was not an ecclesiastical tribunal, and there is nothing in the whole address to imply that the speaker was upon his trial. The truth seems rather to have been that the members of the Council invited him to declare and enforce his opinions concerning the mass before an audience which filled the great church of St. Nicholas.

The argument of his discourse on this occasion was an amplification of the following syllogism: "all worshipping, honouring, or service, invented by the brain of man, in the religion of God, without His express commandment is idolatry: the mass is invented by the brain of man without any commandment of God; therefore, the mass is idolatry." The ground here taken was identical with that which he had defended against Arbuckle, and is distinctively different from the position which, in the very same year, was taken by Cranmer in his "Defence of the true Catholic Doctrine of the Sacrament." The Anglican primate meant by idolatry the substitution of a false God for the true, as in the adoration of the host, for the real body, blood, soul and divinity of the Lord Jesus Christ. But by the same term, as his major premise makes abundantly evident, Knox designated that which we should call now constructive idolatry, namely, "the invention of strange worshippings of God, introduced without any warrant from His word;" or what the Westminster divines meant, when in their Shorter Catechism in answer to the {44} question, "What is forbidden in the second commandment?" they reply, "The worshipping of God by images, or any other way not appointed in His word." With Cranmer the word meant the worshipping as God of that which is no God; with Knox it denoted the worshipping of God in a manner invented by men and unauthorized by God. Cranmer was the father of the Anglican churchmen; Knox was the earliest, and by no means the least noteworthy, of the Puritans, for the principle which he advocated was one which he was as ready to apply to ceremonies in the reformed churches as to the idolatries of the Romish worship. The utterance of these sentiments by him at this time marks the beginning of that movement which has continued even until now, and which in its progress, among other less conspicuous results, called into existence the various nonconforming churches of England; inspired the covenanters of Scotland to begin and carry through their long and painful struggle with the second Charles; widened the civil liberties of Great Britain; and planted the seed from which the American Republic has grown into stateliness and strength.

Its more immediate personal effect, as we have conjectured, was the transference of Knox from Berwick to Newcastle, where he continued to administer word and sacraments in the same manner as he had been accustomed to follow. On the banks of the Tyne he was as faithful and fearless in his pulpit utterances, and as simple in his ritual observances, as he had been on the {45} banks of the Tweed. "God is witness," said he in a letter to his Newcastle friends, written by him from the continent in 1558; "and I refuse not your own judgments, how simply and uprightly I conversed and walked among you, that neither for fear did I spare to speak the simple truth unto you; neither for hope of worldly promotion, dignity, or honour, did I wittingly adulterate any part of God's Scriptures, whether it were in exposition, in preaching, contention, or writing; but that simply and plainly, as it pleased the merciful goodness of my God to give unto me the utterance, understanding, and spirit, I did distribute the bread of life, as of Christ Jesus I had received it;"[1] and again, "How oft have ye assisted to baptism? How oft have ye been partakers of the Lord's Table prepared, and used, and ministered, in all simplicity, not as a man had devised, neither as the king's proceedings did allow, but as Christ Jesus did institute, and as it is evident that Saint Paul did practise?"[2] How it came that he was permitted to administer the sacrament in that manner does not appear; but the fact that he did so is incontrovertible, and that he did not stand quite alone in taking such a course is evident from these words in Becon's "Displaying of the Mass," written in the reign of Queen Mary: "How oft have I seen here, in England, people sitting at the Lord's Table!" It is well known also that the opinions of Hooper, on this subject, were in full accord with those of Knox; and though we have not been able {46} to find any distinct statement that he had actually reduced them to practice, yet it is all but certain that he did so.

But in any case his nonconformity in the matter of kneeling did not keep Knox from attaining a prominent place among the leaders of his time, for in December, 1551, six months after he had been stationed at Newcastle, he was appointed one of King Edward the Sixth's chaplains, who were six in number, and all of whom were selected because they were "accounted the most zealous and ready preachers of that time." This preferment was a recognition of the ability which Knox had shown. It added much to his consideration and weight in the social scale, while it gave him an opportunity of making his influence felt in ecclesiastical affairs in a manner which has left its mark on the English Prayer-Book even until the present day. To understand how this came about, it is needful to bear in mind that the Second or Revised Book of Common Prayer was completed at the press in August, 1552, and had been appointed by the Parliament of that year to come into use in the churches on the first day of November. Into that book had been reintroduced from the "order of communion," published in 1548,[3] {47} the injunction that the people should receive the bread and wine "kneeling." That had, indeed, been the accustomed posture before, but no instruction for its observance had been contained in the First Prayer-Book published in 1549. There the directions are thus given: "Then shall the priest first receive the communion in both kinds himself, and next deliver it to other ministers, if any be there present (that they may be ready to help the chief minister), and after to the people." But in the two years immediately following the publication of that First Prayer-Book, discussion on the posture at the Lord's Table had been brought up, and as Cranmer, Ridley, and the most of the other Reforming Bishops were opposed to the views and practices of Knox, Hooper, and others, they deemed it advisable to foreclose debate and put an end to diversity of order by an authoritative injunction. For this purpose, in the Prayer-Book in 1552 the rubric was made to read thus: "Then shall the minister first receive the communion in both kinds himself, and next deliver it to the other {48} ministers, if any be there present (that they may help the chief minister), and after to the people, in their hands, kneeling." Thus it came about that what had been left undefined in the former book was expressly limited in the new one; and, therefore, though in other respects the latter was much more in harmony with the sentiments of Knox, it was in this less tolerant than the former. When, therefore, Knox was appointed to preach before the king in the autumn of that year, having probably seen one of the first-issued copies of the book, he took occasion to enter fully into the discussion of the mode of administering the communion, and his discourse was not without immediate effect, for in a letter of John Utenhovius to Henry Bullinger, dated October 12, 1552, the writer says:[4] "Some disputes have arisen among the bishops, within these few days, in consequence of a sermon by a pious preacher, chaplain to the Duke of Northumberland, preached by him, before the king and Council, in which he inveighed with great freedom against kneeling at the Lord's Supper, which is still retained here in England. This good man, however, a Scotsman by nation, has so wrought upon the minds of many that we may hope some good to the church will at length arise from it, which I earnestly implore the Lord to grant." Now there can be no doubt that the preacher here referred to was Knox, who as having been in contact with Northumberland as Warden-General of the border counties, might easily be {49} mistaken by a foreigner for the chaplain of that nobleman. Other facts to be taken in connection with the information furnished by Utenhovius are the following:[5] In the Record of the Privy Council, under date 26th September, 1552, there is an order to Grafton, the printer, forbidding him to issue any copies of the new Prayer-Book; and commanding that if any had been already distributed to his fellow-publishers they should "not be put abroad until certain faults therein had been corrected." Clearly therefore, as copies of the book had been sold, it was possible for Knox to have obtained one, and as Lorimer says, "none would be more eager purchasers than those ministers of the Church who were most zealous for reform." Meetings of the Council were held on October 4th and 6th, at one or other of which objections to the rubric seem to have been made, probably as the result of Knox's sermon, and to have been referred to Cranmer for his review. On October 7th, Cranmer wrote to the Council in vindication of the rubric on kneeling, a letter which purports to be a reply to certain objections against it which had been forwarded to him by its members. On the agenda paper of the business to be transacted at the meeting of the Council on the 20th of October, and which still exists in the handwriting of Cecil, there is a line to this effect: "Mr. Knocks--b of Cat|rb|--ye book in ye B of Durh|m|," and at that very meeting, as we learn from the Record, "a letter was directed to Messrs. Harley, Bill, Horn, {50} Grindal, Pern, and Knox, to consider certain articles exhibited to the King's Majesty, to be subscribed by all such as shall be admitted to be preachers or ministers in any part of the realm, and to make report of their opinions touching the same." These articles, therefore, must have come at this time into Knox's hands, and, though many of them must have received his cordial endorsement, there was one of them which he could not have approved; that, namely, which contained this clause: "and as to the character of the ceremonies, they are repugnant in nothing to the wholesome liberty of the gospel, if they are judged from their own nature, but very well agree with it, and in very many respects further the same in a high degree." How could Knox, after his recent sermon on kneeling in the Lord's Supper, give his sanction to that article? Manifestly he would feel that he must protest against such an assertion as it contained; and then, as Lorimer says, "the thought would seem to have flashed upon him that he had now another and quite an unexpected opportunity of making a fresh appeal to the king and Council on that very question of the rubric on kneeling, which was still apparently in dependence. There was still time to make one more attempt. In addition to his judgment upon the articles at large, which need not go to the Council so quickly, what if he should single out this 38th Article and make it the subject of a separate representation, and distinguishing between the ceremony of kneeling and all the rest; what if he should confine the bulk {51} of his representations to this single point, which was now the only one in which it was feasible to look for any immediate alteration?" That at least was done by the memorial, which by its authors is called their confession in regard to the 38th Article, and which Lorimer has printed for the first time in his appendix. No names are subscribed to the document, but the first portion of it bears strong internal evidence of having been the production of Knox; and though in other parts there are traces, as the painstaking editor thinks, of the hands of Thomas Becon and Roger Hutchinson, we agree with him in believing that every one who examines the whole statement with care will conclude "that whatever Englishman may have joined him in the memorial, and whatever they may have contributed to its substance of thought, it was Knox himself who held the pen." This memorial could have been of no use after the final action of the Council on the matter of "kneeling;" and it was evidently called forth by the reference of the articles to the royal chaplains, therefore it must have been prepared between the 20th and 27th October, and must have been presented to the meeting of the Council on the latter of these two dates, on which also, and we may conclude as the result of the arguments contained in the memorial, the "Declaration on Kneeling," which has all the marks of the style of Cranmer, and which therefore had probably been sent by him to the Council as a suggested compromise, was adopted, and ordered to be {52} inserted in the forthcoming book. This accounts for the circumstance mentioned by the editor of "The Two Liturgies" in a note, that the paragraph in question "is printed on a separate leaf in some copies, and as is evident from the signatures, was added afterwards." In one copy, "the leaf is pasted in after the copy was bound, and several copies are without it." Now putting all these things together, the conclusion is not only legitimate but inevitable, that the insertion of the declaration on kneeling in the Prayer-Book was due to the agency of Knox, more probably than to that of any other man. As Lorimer writes (p. 121), "The compromise prevailed, but apparently there would not have been so much as a compromise obtained if the 'confession' had not been thrown into the scale at the very last moment.... His last blow had the effect of overcoming the resistance to all further change which a majority of the Council had hitherto maintained." Hence, though we may not approve of the spirit in which Weston uttered the words, or accept either his description of Knox or his designation of the doctrine on which he insisted, yet he was correct as to the matter of fact when he said, "a renegade Scot did take away the adoration and worshipping of Christ in the sacrament, by whose procurement that heresy was put into the last communion book; so much prevailed that one man's authority at that time."

The Declaration itself was in the following words:--"Although no order can be so perfectly devised, but it {53} may be of some, either for their ignorance and infirmity, or else of malice and obstinacy, misconstrued, depraved, and interpreted in a wrong part: And yet, because brotherly charity willeth, that so much as conveniently may be, offences should be taken away; therefore we willing to do the same: Whereas it is ordained in the Book of Common Prayer, in the administration of the Lord's Supper, that the communicants kneeling should receive the Holy Communion: which thing being well meant, for a signification of the humble and grateful acknowledging of the benefits of Christ, given unto the worthy receiver, and to avoid the profanation and disorder, which about the Holy Communion might else ensue: lest yet the same kneeling might be thought or taken otherwise, we do declare that it is not meant thereby, that any adoration is done, or ought to be done, either unto the sacramental bread and wine there bodily received, or to any real and essential presence there being of Christ's natural flesh and blood. For as concerning the sacramental bread and wine, they remain still in their very natural substances, and therefore may not be adored, for that were Idolatry to be abhorred of all faithful Christians. And as concerning the natural body and blood of our Saviour Christ they are in heaven and not here. For it is against the truth of Christ's true natural body, to be in more places than in one at one time." Opinions will of course differ as to whether in this matter the influence of Knox was beneficial or the reverse. We are writing biography, not a treatise on {54} theology, and what we have been seeking to show is the share that Knox had in the English Reformation. Sacramentarians generally will agree in styling the Declaration which we have quoted "the black rubric," but for ourselves we have no hesitation in avowing our agreement with Lorimer that "there is nothing in the whole English Liturgy which is, to say the least, more Protestant;" and it may be well, to give completeness to our reference to the subject, that we should add that author's very condensed summary of the subsequent history of this famous rubric. "At the accession of Elizabeth it was dropped out of the Prayer-Book, along with that portion of the 35th Article upon which it rested; and it remained outside the Liturgy for a hundred years. And why? Simply because its omission was judged as important by the Church's leaders then as its insertion had been at first. Elizabeth's church policy was a comprehensive policy, and neither James I. nor Charles I. had any wish to depart from it. She wished, and so did her council and first Parliament, to make it as easy as possible for the "Roman party to continue in the National Church, but she and they knew that such a comprehension was impossible as long as the "Declaration on Kneeling" remained in the Prayer-Book. Its insertion had taken place in order to "comprehend" the Puritan party, to the exclusion of the Romanists; and now its omission took place in order to comprehend the Romanists, at the risk of driving out the Puritans. But why do we now {55} find the "Declaration" restored to its old place? What was the motive of so remarkable a rehabilitation in 1662? It is easy to discern it. The circle of church evolution and change had then returned into itself. In 1662 the old policy of conciliating and comprehending the Puritans instead of the Catholics was again in season--was again the key of the situation. To this policy the "Declaration on Kneeling" was again indispensable, and again, therefore, this most remarkable rubric was restored, in substantially the same form, to its vacant place. Nor has its history yet exhausted itself. It has retained its recovered place through all the changes of the last two centuries only to come forward into new significance and importance in our own day. The last chapter of its history was written only the other day in the long discussion and the fateful decision of the Bennett case. Its simple but trenchant language was often quoted in the pleadings, and passed into the body of the judgment itself: "As concerning the natural body and blood of our Saviour Christ they are in heaven, not here: for it is against the truth of Christ's true natural body to be in more places than in one at one time."

But the memorial to the Privy Council, which we have traced to Knox, prevailed also so far as to secure a modification of the article on ceremonies, which, originally numbered as the 38th, came out owing to some minor condensations as the 35th, and took this ultimate shape--(we give Lorimer's translation from {56} the Latin)--"The book which of very late time was given to the Church of England by the king's authority and the Parliament, containing the manner and form of praying and ministering the sacraments in the Church of England, likewise also the book of ordering ministers of the Church set forth by the foresaid authority, are godly, and in no point repugnant to the wholesome doctrine of the gospel, but agreeable thereunto, furthering and beautifying the same not a little; and therefore of all faithful members of the Church of England, and chiefly of the ministers of the Lord, they ought to be received and allowed with all readiness of mind and thanksgiving, and to be commended to the people of God."[6] When this is compared with the clause formerly given it will be seen that what before was said of the "ceremonies" is here restricted to the "doctrine," and that everything to which the memorial had taken exception is omitted.

But though the insertion of the Declaration on Kneeling into the Prayer-Book satisfied one of the conditions which, in his letter to his Berwick friends, Knox had laid down as essential to his conforming to "common Order": it did not meet the others, and so he steadily refused to accept a formal charge in the Church of England. At the very time when the Council was {57} engaged in the discussions which we have just mentioned, the Duke of Northumberland wrote from Chelsea, under date October 27th, 1552, to Secretary Cecil, in these words:[7] "I would to God it might please the King's majesty to appoint Mr. Knox to the office of Rochester bishopric, which for three reasons would be very well. First: he would not only be a whetstone to quicken and sharp the Bishop of Canterbury, whereof he hath need, but also would be a great confounder of the Anabaptists lately sprung up in Kent. Secondly, he should not continue the ministration in the north, contrary to this set forth here" (meaning to the usual form prescribed at this time). "Thirdly, the family of the Scots now inhabiting in Newcastle, chiefly for his fellowship, would not continue there, wherein many resort to them out of Scotland, which is not requisite." These are certainly rather strange reasons why Knox should be promoted to a bishopric, but they prove not only that he had acted an independent part in Newcastle, but also that his fame had gone so widely over Scotland that multitudes of his fellow-countrymen were attracted to that place for the sake of enjoying his ministrations. But he would not be made a bishop, and he must have expressed his refusal with all his wonted plainness of speech, for a few weeks later, on the 7th December, Northumberland writes to the same correspondent: "Master Knox's being here to speak with me, saying he was so willed by you; I do return him again, {58} because I love not to have to do with men which be neither grateful nor pleasable."[8] So his grace is minded to put the case; but with his former letter in our hands we can see that gratitude in his vocabulary meant falling in with his individual plans, and "pleasableness" was with him a synonym for "squeezeableness."

In the following February (1553) Knox was offered the Vicarage of All Hallows in Bread Street (London); but that also he declined, and we have from the pen of Calderwood an account of what occurred in connection with that.[9] "In a letter, dated the 14th of April, 1553, and written with his own hand, I find," says that author, "that he was called before the Council of England for kneeling, who demanded of him three questions. First, why he refused the benefice provided for him? secondly, whether he thought that no Christian might serve in the ecclesiastical ministration according to the rites and laws of the realm of England? thirdly, if kneeling at the Lord's Table was not indifferent? To the first he answered, that his conscience did witness that he might profit more in some other place than in London; and therefore had no pleasure to accept any office in the same. Howbeit, he might have answered otherwise, that he refused that parsonage because of my Lord of Northumberland's command. To the second, that many things were worthy of reformation in the ministry of England, without the reformation whereof no minister {59} did discharge, or could discharge, his conscience before God; for no minister in England had authority to divide and separate the lepers from the whole, which was a chief point of his office; yet did he not refuse such office as might appear to promote God's glory in utterance of Christ's gospel in a mean degree, where more he might edify by preaching of the true word than hinder by sufferance of manifest iniquity, seeing that reformation of manners did not appertain to all ministers. To the third he answered, that Christ's action in itself was most perfect, and Christ's action was done without kneeling; that kneeling was man's addition or imagination; that it was most sure to follow the example of Christ, whose action was done sitting and not kneeling. In this last question there was great contention betwixt the whole table of the lords and him. There were present there the Bishops of Canterbury and Ely, my Lord Treasurer, the Marquis of Northampton, the Earl of Bedford, the Earl of Shrewsbury, Master Comptroller, my Lord Chamberlain, both the Secretaries, and other inferior lords. After long reasoning, it was said unto him that he was not called of any evil mind; that they were sorry to know him of a contrary mind to the common Order. He answered that he was more sorry that a common Order should be contrary to Christ's institution. With some gentle speeches he was dismissed, and willed to advise with himself if he would communicate after that Order." But, unlike Hooper, who, after a long controversy about vestments and a brief {60} imprisonment for his refusal to wear them, accepted the bishopric of Gloucester, vestments and all, only however to suffer martyrdom at last under Queen Mary, Knox remained steadfast to the position which he had taken up; and, refusing a permanent charge, which would have required him to give his assent and consent to the Articles, and to conform to the common Order, he was sent in June, 1553, as one of the itinerary preachers into Buckinghamshire, where he laboured with great zeal and assiduity for some weeks.

In the interval between October, 1552, and March, 1553, we find that Knox had been back at Newcastle, where he was bitterly opposed by Sir Robert Brandling, the Mayor, whose zeal was checked, however, by the agency of Lord Wharton, then Lord Warden of the North, at the suggestion of Northumberland; and there are some interesting letters belonging to this portion of his life which give us delightful glimpses into his heart and habits. In one we see him "sitting at his book," and contemplating Matthew's Gospel by the help of "some most godly expositions, and among the rest Chrysostom." In another he writes, "This day ye know to be the day of my study and prayer to God." And in a third, written to Mrs. Bowes from London, whither he had been summoned in haste before the Privy Council, we have this record: "The very instant hour that your letters were presented unto me was I talking of you, by reason that three honest poor women were come to me, and were complaining their great infirmity, and were {61} showing unto me the great assaults of the enemy, and I was opening the causes and commodities thereof, whereby all our eyes wept at once; and I was praying unto God that you and some others had been there with me for the space of two hours, and even at that instant came your letters to my hands, whereof the part I read unto them; and one of them said, 'Oh would to God I might speak with that person, for I perceive there be more tempted than I.'" Thus amid the multiplicity and weight of his public labours he did not neglect either the study or the closet; and the weeping Knox, seeking to comfort those that were cast down, is a picture that must seem strange to many who know little more about him than that his fortitude made Mary Stuart shed tears of wounded pride and disappointed ambition.

In April he preached in the Chapel Royal before the young king, and inveighed in the strongest terms against Northumberland and Paulet, finishing one of his scathing passages in this way: "Was David and Hezekiah, princes of great and godly gifts and experience, abused by crafty counsellors and dissembling hypocrites? What wonder is it, then, that a young and innocent king be deceived by crafty, covetous, wicked, and ungodly counsellors? I am greatly afraid that Ahithophel be councillor, that Judas bear the purse, and that Shebna be scribe, comptroller and treasurer." The pulpit in those days had to discharge the duties of public criticism on politics and morals, which are now much more appropriately performed by the press; and so, as Froude {62} remarks, "since discipline could not be restored, Knox, and those who felt with him the enormities of the times, established, by their own authority, this second form of excommunication." It was then perhaps a necessity, but it is always, more or less, a dangerous thing for a minister to do; and it must be admitted that Knox was not always just in such philippics. But he was always conscientious, and he was always brave; and he well knew at the moment the risk which he was running. In the present case, if little good came out of it to the country, no harm resulted from it to himself; for, as we have seen, he was shortly afterwards engaged to preach in Buckinghamshire. And there he laboured on, like another Jeremiah, forecasting evils which none of his hearers would believe could happen, until at the death of Edward the Sixth, on the 6th of July, 1553, they were rudely awakened from their sleep of security.

Such was Knox's share in the working out of the English Reformation; and we have dwelt thus long upon it because the facts which we have stated have only recently been brought to light; and because we wished to set forth with as much clearness as condensation would allow the opinions which were held, and the mode of worship which was observed, by him, even at this early stage in his history. If Knox did something for England, England did much also for him. If he was instrumental in keeping the Church of that country from greater affinity with Romanism than it might otherwise have shown, there can be no doubt that the evil effects {63} of compromise as witnessed by him there helped to make him more thorough in his later work in Scotland; while it is also most true that during his residence there his contact with the Christian people whom he met did something to soften and sweeten his piety, and to make it more inward and sympathising. Most of all, God was preparing him by it for the great work which he was afterwards to perform in his native land; and his years of service in England were blessed in securing for him the friendship and confidence of her ablest statesmen, without whose assistance, humanly speaking, Scotland might have been lost to Protestantism in the very crisis of her history.

[1] Lorimer, p. 73.

[2] Ibid., p. 74.

[3] Dr. Lorimer has said (p. 31) that "in both the formularies recently set forth," the Order of Communion in 1548 and the "Book of Common Prayer" in 1549, the practice of kneeling in the Lord's Supper had been retained; and on a subsequent page (112) that "in the Second Prayer-Book of King Edward VI. a rubric had for the first time been inserted appointing the Lord's Supper to be administered to the communicants in a kneeling posture." But these statements are not made with that author's usual accuracy. For the "Order of Communion" reads thus: "Then shall the priest rise, the people still reverently kneeling, and the priest shall deliver the communion, first to the ministers, if any be there present, that they may help the chief minister, and after to the others." But in the "Book" of 1549, the rubric is as we give it in the text. What the motive was for the omission of kneeling in the Book of 1549 it is not easy to say, but the fact of its omission is undoubted. (See "The Two Liturgies," by Rev. Joseph Kelley, p. 92.)

[4] Lorimer, p. 98.

[5] Lorimer, p. 109.

[6] For the full discussion of this subject we refer to Dr. Lorimer's monograph, "John Knox and the Church of England," a most valuable and original contribution to English Ecclesiastical history, though the absence of an index makes it less serviceable to the student than such a work should be.

[7] Lorimer, pp. 149-150.

[8] Lorimer, p. 151.

[9] See Laing: "Knox's Works," vol. iii. pp. 86-7.

CHAPTER V.

LAST DAYS IN ENGLAND, 1553.

During the last illness of the young King Edward, Knox, as we have seen, received a commission to go upon a preaching tour in the county of Buckingham, where, like an old Hebrew prophet, he warned his hearers of the coming crisis. He was back in London, however, as we learn from the date of the first of his published letters, on the 23rd of June (1553); but before the death of his majesty, which happened on the 6th of July, he had returned to Buckinghamshire, and there, at Amersham, on the 16th of that month, he preached a sermon suited to the times in the very thick of the turmoil caused by the dispute as to the succession to the crown. The Duke of Northumberland had presumed to set the Lady Jane Dudley on the throne, but Mary Tudor's adherents could not brook such disloyalty to their mistress, and had already entered on that struggle which ended in the collapse of the reign of "the twelfth-day Queen." The county of Bucks, as Froude tells us, "both Catholic and Protestant," was "arming to the teeth." Sir Edward Hastings had called {65} out its musters, in Mary's name, and had been joined by Peckham, the cofferer of the royal household, who had gone off with the treasure under his charge, so that the Reformer was speaking "at the peril of his life among the troopers of Hastings." Nevertheless, nothing daunted, he thus apostrophised the land:[1] "O England! now is God's wrath kindled against thee. Now hath He begun to punish as He hath threatened a long while by His true prophets and messengers. He hath taken from thee the crown of thy glory, and hath left thee without honour as a body without a head. And this appeareth to be only the beginning of sorrows, which appeareth to increase. For I perceive that the heart, the tongue, and the hand of one Englishman is bent against another, and division to be in the whole realm, which is an assured sign of desolation to come. O England! England! dost thou not consider that thy commonwealth is like a ship sailing on the sea; if thy mariners and governors shall one consume another, shalt thou not suffer shipwreck in short process of time? O England! England! alas these plagues are poured upon thee, for that thou wouldest not know the most happy time of thy gentle visitation. But wilt thou yet obey the voice of thy God and submit thyself to His holy words? Truly if thou wilt, thou shalt find mercy in His sight, and the estate of thy commonwealth shall be preserved. But if thou obstinately wilt return into Egypt, that is, if thou contract marriage, confederacy, and league with such {66} princes as do maintain and advance idolatry (such as the Emperor, which is no less enemy unto Christ than ever was Nero); if for the pleasure and friendship (I say) of such princes them return to thine old abominations, before used under the papistry, then assuredly, O England, thou shall be plagued and brought to desolation by the means of those whose favour thou seekest, and by whom thou art procured to fall from Christ and to serve Antichrist." These were bold words. Some of them, indeed, might be called rash, and, as we shall see, furnished a weapon for his adversaries at a future day; but there was no quailing in the heart of him who uttered them, and the sting of them after all was in their truth.

From Amersham he went up to London, where on the 19th of July he was a witness of the great outburst of popular enthusiasm with which Mary was welcomed to the throne; but he could not share in the wild delight of the multitude, for as he tells us himself, "in London, in more places than one, when fires of joy and riotous banqueting were at the proclamation of Mary," his tongue was vehement in declaring his forebodings of the storm which was so soon to break. On the 26th of July he wrote to Mrs. Bowes from Carlisle, and again on the 25th of September we find him writing to her on his return to London from Kent, where he seems to have been labouring for some weeks. The dates indicate that he was both "in labours abundant" and "in journeyings often," and show that he had little reason to {67} upbraid himself, as in one of his writings referring to this time he does, for "allowing the love of friends and carnal affection for some men more than others to allure him to make more residence in one place than another, thus having more respect to the pleasure of a few than to the necessity of many, and not sufficiently considering how many hungry souls were in other places to whom none took pains to break and distribute the bread of life." But he was ere long to be "in peril" as well as labour. From the first he had augured nothing but evil from the accession of Mary, and it is to his honour that with such misgivings in his heart, he was at this very time in the habit of using in the pulpit a prayer of singular beauty and comprehensiveness, in which we find this petition: "Illuminate the heart of our Sovereign Lady Queen Mary with pregnant gifts of the Holy Ghost, and influence the hearts of her council with Thy true fear and love." As the months rolled round, however, it became only too apparent that England would no longer be a safe place for him. The door of opportunity which Edward had opened was speedily closed by Mary. In August, indeed, she issued a proclamation giving toleration to all meanwhile, forbidding her Protestant and Catholic subjects to interrupt each other's services, yet prohibiting all preaching on either side without licence from herself. But in November, under the influence of the violent reaction which had set in, and in obedience to the opinion of the people, three-fourths of whom were still attached to the old religion, the {68} Commons, by a vote of 350 to 80, enacted that from the 20th December following there should be no other form of service in the churches but what had been used in the last year of Henry the Eighth, and leaving it free to all up till that date to use either of the books appointed by Edward or the old one at their pleasure. Up till the day thus specified, therefore, Knox was comparatively safe, and during that time he was probably in London a guest in the families of the Lockes and the Hickmans, with whose members he afterwards corresponded. It was in this interval also, as seems most probable, that he began to prepare his exposition of the sixth Psalm, and his "godly letter to the faithful in London, Newcastle, Berwick, and all others within the realm of England that love the coming of our Lord Jesus Christ," both of which were afterwards finished in France.

From London he went to Newcastle, whence on the 22nd of December he wrote to Mrs. Bowes a letter which contains a postscript to this effect: "I may not answer the places of Scripture, nor yet write the exposition of the sixth Psalm, for every day of this week must I preach, if this wicked carcase will permit." But dangers began to thicken around him; for in the end of December or beginning of January, his servant was seized as he carried letters from him to Mrs. Bowes and her daughter, in the expectation of finding something in them that might furnish matter of accusation against him. They contained nothing but religious advices and such things as he was prepared to avow before any {69} tribunal in the country, but fearing that the report of the matter might cause uneasiness to his friends at Berwick, he set out to visit them in person. On the way, however, he was met by some of the relatives of his betrothed, who prevailed on him to relinquish his intention, and to retire to a place of safety on the coast, from which, if necessary, he might escape out of the country by sea. From this retreat he wrote to his friends, saying that "his brethren had, partly by tears and partly by admonition, compelled him to obey, somewhat contrary to his own mind, for never could he die in a more honest quarrel than by suffering as a witness for that truth of which God had made him a messenger," yet promising if Providence prepared the way to do as his counsellors advised, and "give place to the fury and rage of Satan for a time." So when he became satisfied that the apprehensions of his friends were, well founded, he procured a vessel which landed him safely at Dieppe on the 20th of January, 1554. What his pecuniary circumstances at this time were may be inferred from these words in a letter to his future mother-in-law: "I will not make you privy how rich I am, but off (i.e. from) London I departed with less money than ten groats; but God has since provided, and will provide I doubt not hereafter abundantly for this life. Either the Queen's Majesty or some treasurer will be forty pounds richer by me, for so much lack I of duty of my patents (that is, salary as Royal Chaplain), but that little troubles me." And more interesting even than that glimpse {70} into his poverty is the recital of his feelings toward England in a letter to the same correspondent written just before his embarkation: "My daily prayer is for the sore afflicted in those quarters. Some time I have thought that it had been impossible so to have removed my affection from Scotland that any realm or nation could have been equally dear unto me; but I take God to record in my conscience that the troubles present and appearing to be in the realm of England are doubly more dolorous unto my heart than ever were the troubles of Scotland."

Thus Knox parted from the realm of England. Had he remained much longer in it, he would most probably have shared the fate of Cranmer, Ridley, Latimer, and the "noble army," whom Mary's intolerance "chased up to heaven." But God had other work for him to do, and it was well for Scotland that he listened to the entreaty of those who counselled him when he was "persecuted in one country" to "flee to another"; so it came about that for a brief season he found refuge in that land wherein only a few years before he had been a galley-slave.

CHAPTER VI.

FIRST DAYS OF EXILE, 1554.

From England Knox went to Dieppe, where he sojourned at this time for a month, and finished his exposition of the sixth Psalm, the first instalment of which he had sent to Mrs. Bowes just before leaving the shores of Britain. This production was primarily designed for the consolation and encouragement of that lady, who, as we have already hinted, seems to have been afflicted with religious melancholy. Apparently she was one of those, of whom every pastor has had some experience, who believe that God has cast them off, and who while "fearing the Lord," yet "walk in darkness and have no light." Her life was one constant wrestle with spiritual depression, by which her intimate friends were afflicted almost as much as she was herself. Knox dealt with her most tenderly, and under the influence of his wise words she regained her comfort for a time, but after a little she was in the depths again, and the whole process had to be gone over with her anew. Had she lived in modern days, a prudent friend would have counselled her to consult a skilful physician, {72} and would have sought to combine medical treatment with religious advice. We cannot wonder, however, that we have nothing in this tractate bearing on that aspect of the matter. The writer deals throughout with the malady as spiritual, but he treats it most wisely, and the great well of tenderness in his heart reveals itself to the reader in such a passage as the following:[1] "These things put I you in mind of, beloved mother, that albeit your pains sometimes be so horrible that no release nor comfort ye find neither in spirit nor yet in body, yet if the heart can only sob unto God, despair not, you shall obtain your heart's desire, and destitute you are not of faith. For at such time as the flesh, natural reason, the law of God, the present torment, and the devil at once do cry God is angry, and therefore is there neither help nor remedy to be hoped for at His hands; at such time, I say, to sob unto God is the demonstration of the secret seed of God which is hid in God's elect children, and that only sob is unto God a more acceptable sacrifice than, without this cross, to give our bodies to be burned even for the truth's sake." Very comprehensive also is this expansion of the second petition of the Lord's Prayer in the same treatise.[2] "We are commanded daily to pray, 'Thy kingdom come,' which petition asketh that sin may cease, that death may be devoured, that transitory troubles may have an end, that Satan may be trodden under our feet, that the whole {73} body of Christ may be restored to life, liberty, and joy, that the powers and kingdoms of this earth may be dissolved and destroyed, and that God the Father may be all in all things, after that His Son Christ Jesus, the Saviour, hath rendered up the kingdom for ever." And in these days when so much is written, both wise and otherwise, on the subject of eschatology, some interest may be felt in the following "bit" of exposition. "'For there is no remembrance of Thee in death;

who laudeth Thee in the pit?' As (if) David would say, 'O Lord, how shall I pray and declare Thy goodness when I am dead, and gone into the grave? It is not the ordinary course to have Thy miracles and wondrous works preached unto men by those that are buried and gone down into the pit. Those that are dead make no mention of Thee in the earth, and therefore, O Lord, spare Thy servant, that yet for a time I may show and witness Thy wondrous works unto mankind.' These most godly affections in David did engender in him a vehement horror and fear of death, besides that which is natural and common to all men, because he perfectly understood that by death he shall be lettit (hindered) any further to advance the glory of God. Of the same he complaineth most vehemently in the 88th Psalm, where apparently he taketh from them that are dead, sense, remembrance, feeling, and understanding, alleging that God worketh no miracles by the dead, that the goodness of God cannot be preached in the grave, nor His faith in perdition, and that His marvellous works {74} are not known in darkness. By which speeches we may not understand that David taketh all sense and feeling from the dead, neither yet that they who are dead in Christ are in such estate that by God they have not consolation and life. No; Christ Himself doth witness the contrary. But David so vehemently depresses their estate and condition, because that after death they are deprived from (of) all ordinary ministration in the Kirk of God. None of those that are departed are appointed to be preachers of God's glory unto mankind. But after death they cease any more to advance God's holy name here among the living on earth, and so shall even they in that behalf be unprofitable to the congregation as touching anything that they can do, either in body or soul after death. And therefore most earnestly desired David to live in Israel for the further manifestation of God's glory."[3]

Appended to this tract there is the date "upon the very point of my journey, the last of February, 1553(4), so that Knox left Dieppe about the beginning of March, but before his departure he finished and transmitted the first of that series of admonitions and consolatory epistles which during his exile on the continent he addressed to his friends in England, and from which we have already quoted so many passages throwing light upon his labours among them. This earliest of the series is entitled "A Godly Letter of Warning or Admonition to the Faithful in London, Newcastle, and Berwick," {75} and is written in a strain of burning and impassioned expostulation. It is mainly founded on the sermon preached by Jeremiah to the princes and all the people of Judah in the beginning of the reign of Jehoiakim, as recorded in the

26th chapter of his prophecies. Knox runs a skilful parallel between the circumstances of the Jews before the destruction of their capital by Nebuchadnezzar, and those of the people of England under Mary, and with the presage of coming judgment darkening his spirit, he exhorts the "remnant" to fidelity and earnestness. One extract will give the reader some slight idea of its style and purport. [4]"Hitherto have I recited the estate of Judah before the destruction of Jerusalem and subversion of that commonwealth. Now I appeal to the conscience of any indifferent (i.e. impartial) man in what one point differ the manners, estate and regiment (i.e. government) of England this day from the abuse and estate rehearsed of Judah in these days, except that they had a king, a man of his own nature (as appeared), more facile than cruel, who sometimes was entreated in the prophet's favour, and also in some cases heard his counsel; and ye have a queen, a woman of a stout stomach (i.e. of a haughty spirit), more stiff in opinion than flexible to the truth, who no wise may abide the presence of God's prophets. In this one thing you disagree; in all other things as like as one bean or nut is like to another, (1) Their king was led by pestilent priests; who guides your queen, it is not {76} unknown. (2) Under Zedekiah and his council the idolatry which by Josiah was suppressed, came to light again; but more abominable idolatry was never in the earth than is that which of late is now set up again by your pestilent papists among you. (3) In Jerusalem was Jeremiah persecuted and cast into prison for speaking the truth and rebuking their idolatry; what prison in London tormenteth not some true prophet of God for the same causes? And O thou dungeon of darkness, where that abominable idol of late days was first erected (thou Tower of London, I mean), in thee are tormented more Jeremiahs than one, whom God shall comfort according to His promise, and shall reward their persecutors even as they have deserved; in which day also shalt thou tremble for fear, and such as pretend to defend thee shall perish with thee, because thou wast first defiled with that abominable idol."

The letter concludes with the following touching sentences:--"The peace of God rest with you all. From one sore troubled heart upon my departure from Dieppe--1553(4)--whither God knoweth. In God is my trust, through Jesus Christ His Son; and therefore I fear not the tyranny of man, neither yet what the devil can invent against me. Rejoice, ye faithful, for in joy shall we meet where death may not dissever us."

At the time when he wrote these words he seems to have had no definite purpose as to his immediate destination, but we have now no difficulty in tracing his movements, for in a letter addressed to his afflicted {77} brethren in England, and dated Dieppe, 10th May, 1554, we find the following words:-- "My own estate is this: since the 28th of January I have travelled through all the congregations of Helvetia (Switzerland), and have reasoned with all the pastors and many other excellent learned men upon such matters as now I cannot commit to writing; gladly I would by tongue or by pen utter the same to God's glory." What these things were may perhaps be inferred from the words of Bullinger to Calvin in a letter dated 26th March, 1554, to this effect: "I have enclosed in this letter the answer I made to the Scotsman whom you commended to me; you will return it to me when you have opportunity."[5] Now as Knox visited Geneva in that month of March, and obtained from Calvin a letter of introduction to Bullinger, there can be no doubt, as Dr. Laing has shown, that the reference is to him. The questions which he submitted to Bullinger were the following, and we give them entire, with a brief summary of the answer to each, that we may make plain the gravity and importance of the matters which were at this time engrossing his attention:--(1) "Whether the son of a king, upon his father's death, though unable by reason of his tender age to conduct the government of the kingdom, is nevertheless by right of inheritance to be regarded as a lawful magistrate, and as such to be obeyed as of Divine right?" This, illustrating his statement by a reference to King Edward the Sixth of England, Bullinger answers in the {78} affirmative. (2) "Whether a female can preside over and rule a kingdom by Divine right, and so transfer the right of sovereignty to her husband?" To this Bullinger replies, that, though the law of God ordains the woman to be in subjection, yet as it is a hazardous thing for godly persons to set themselves up in opposition to political regulations, and in the gospel does not seem to unsettle hereditary rights, the people of God may rejoice in a female sovereign if she be like Deborah; and if she be of a different character, they may have an example and consolation in the case of Athaliah; but with respect to the right of transferring the government to her husband, only those persons who are acquainted with the laws and customs of the realm can give a proper answer. (3) "Whether obedience is to be rendered to a magistrate who enforces idolatry and condemns true religion; and whether those authorities who are still in military occupations of towns and fortresses are permitted to repel this ungodly violence from themselves and their friends?" No definite or categorical answer is given to this inquiry, on the ground that it is difficult to pronounce on every particular case; but while there is need of wisdom, lest by rashness and corruption much mischief may be occasioned to many worthy persons, it is unequivocally asserted that death itself is far preferable to the admission of idolatry. (4) "To which party must godly persons attach themselves in the case of a religious nobility resisting an idolatrous sovereign?" This is left by the Swiss Reformer to the judgment of the individual {79} conscience. Between the lines of these questions we can easily read that Knox was pondering questions which lie near the foundation of civil and religious liberty; and that, foreseeing the occasion which he might soon have for dealing practically with them, he availed himself of the opportunity furnished by his exile for consulting the most eminent Swiss Protestant divines regarding them.

He returned to Dieppe in May, 1554, and remained there until the end of July in order that he might gain accurate information concerning his brethren in England, and might learn whether he could do anything in their behalf. To these weeks must be assigned the preparation and transmission of his "Faithful Admonition unto the Professors of God's Truth in England," which caused him so much trouble in the Frankfort episode of his history. For that reason, therefore, it may be well to give a brief account of this trenchant production. It is evidently the expansion of a discourse formerly preached by him on the experience of the disciples in the storm, when they "toiled in rowing" because "the wind was contrary unto them," with a pungent and sometimes not very prudent, application of its lessons to the circumstances which then existed in England. It was his habit to preach his sermons before he wrote them, and indeed, so far as appears, he did not often write them out, even after they had been delivered, but usually contented himself with speaking from a few notes, which were made in the margin of his Bible, and which remained the sole {80} memoranda of the discourse. In the present case the note was to the effect "Videat Anglia"--"Let England beware!" and the matter written in his book in Latin was this: "Seldom it is that God worketh any notable work to the comfort of His Church but that trouble, fear, and labour cometh upon such as God hath used for His servants and His workmen; and also tribulation most commonly followeth that Church where Christ Jesus is most truly preached." In his exposition he goes on to explain why, after the miracle of the feeding of the multitude, Christ sent both the people at large and His disciples away; and dwells on the danger to which the apostles were exposed, the manner of their deliverance through the coming and the word of Christ, the zeal of Peter in seeking to meet the Lord on the waves, and his fear in sinking in the waters, and the mercy of the Master in permitting neither Peter nor the rest of the disciples to perish, but gloriously delivering them all. Into his treatment of these several things he introduces plentiful allusions to the state of affairs in England, and the object which he has before him as a whole is two-fold--first, to encourage those who had made a profession of the Reformed Faith to maintain the beginning of their confidence steadfast unto the end; and second, to give warning of the dangers which were to be apprehended if the kingdom should come under the dominion of strangers, as it would infallibly do when Mary became the wife of Philip of Spain. The admonition bears the imprint "20th day of July, 1554." Now the marriage {81} of Mary to Philip was celebrated on the 25th day of that same month, and it was provided by the treaty for that alliance, and confirmed by Act of Parliament, that Philip, as the husband of Mary, "should have and enjoy, jointly with the Queen his wife, the style, honour, and kingly name of the realm and dominions unto the said Queen appertaining, and shall aid her Highness, being his wife, in the happy administration of her realm and dominions." This helps us to understand one of the questions which Knox had proposed to Bullinger, and explains at least, if it cannot justify, the vehemence of his feelings and the violence of his words in the "admonition." He speaks of "Stephen Gardiner and his black brood;" calls the wafer of the host "the round clipped God;" declares that "the devil rageth in his obedient servants, wily Winchester, dreaming Durham, and bloody Bonner, with the rest of their bloody, butcherly brood;" avers that Jezebel "never erected half so many gallows in all Israel as mischievous Mary hath done within London alone;" denounces Mary as a "breaker of promises;" calls her that most unhappy and wicked woman;" and foretells evil for England if she--i.e. England--contract marriage, confederacy, or league with such princes as do maintain and advance idolatry (such as the Emperor, which is no less an enemy here to Christ than ever was Nero)." All this is dreadful enough. But let us bear in mind that Mary, on her accession, had publicly declared that she "meant graciously not to compel or strain other men's consciences otherwise than God should, as she trusted, {82} put in their hearts a persuasion of the truth, through the opening of His word unto them," and that, by her subsequent conduct she had utterly falsified that word; let it be remembered that at the very time of Knox's writing, Cranmer, Ridley, and Latimer had been prisoners for seven or eight months in the Tower, first under the charge of treason, and latterly under that of heresy; let it be considered that reports were continually coming to Knox's ears of the daily increasing sufferings of the Protestants in England, and then some allowance will be made for the outburst of his indignation in these passionate utterances. Still, when we have made all such allowance, we must admit that a more cautious man would have foreseen that a probable effect of such a bitter onslaught would be the increase of the persecutor's fury, and would not have gone out of his way to irritate the German Emperor by comparing him with Nero. But caution never was one of Knox's distinctive excellences. If it had, he would not have become a Reformer, for your merely cautious men are of very little service either to their generation or to the world. Boldness is necessary for progress, and where the boldness is, we must reconcile ourselves as best we may to its attendant shadow. In the present instance Knox paid dearly enough for his imprudence, as we shall shortly see, and we may therefore content ourselves with this simple reference to it.

[1] "Works," vol. iii. p. 137.

[2] Ibid., p. 128.

[3] "Works," vol. iii. pp. 151-2.

[4] "Works," vol. iii. pp. 187-8.

[5] "Works," vol. iii. pp. 219, 226.

CHAPTER VII.

THE TROUBLES AT FRANKFORT, 1554-1555.

From Dieppe, after having launched across the channel the thunderbolt of the "Faithful Admonition," Knox retired to Geneva, where he enjoyed the friendship of John Calvin and other Swiss divines, and where, though he was now bordering on fifty years of age, he applied himself to the study of Hebrew with all the ardour of youth. But such a man could not long be permitted to enjoy learned leisure. Accordingly we find that in the end of September, 1554, he was called to be one of the pastors of a congregation of English exiles who had found an asylum in Frankfort-on-the-Maine, a city whose inhabitants had early embraced the principles of the Reformation, and befriended refugees from all countries so far as that could be done by them without coming to an open breach with the Emperor. Already a church of French Protestants was in existence there, and on application to the authorities the English exiles obtained the joint use of the place of worship allotted to that congregation, on condition that they should in their {84} service conform as nearly as possible to the forms observed by the French. This was thankfully accepted by the English, who agreed among themselves, be it observed before Knox appeared among them, to give up the audible responses, the Litany, the surplice, and other things which "in these reformed churches would seem more than strange." It is added in the "Brief Discourse of the Troubles begun at Frankfort" which lies before us as we write, that "as touching the ministration of the sacraments, sundry things were also by common consent omitted as superstitious and superfluous;" and that "after that the congregation had thus concluded and agreed, and had chosen their minister and deacons to serve for a time, they entered their church on the 29th of July."

Having thus secured for themselves religious privileges, the Frankfort exiles by a circular letter invited their brethren in other continental cities to come and share the blessing with them. To this the English residents at Strasburg replied recommending certain persons as well qualified to fill the offices of superintendent or bishop, and pastors, but before receiving that communication the brethren at Frankfort had already chosen three persons, one of whom was Knox, to be their pastors, and to be invested with co-ordinate authority. The invitation was not specially attractive to Knox, both because he was loth to sacrifice the advantages for study which he was enjoying at Geneva, and because he feared the outbreak of such a {85} controversy as ultimately arose. But moved by what McCrie has styled "the powerful intercession of Calvin," he accepted the call and went to Frankfort about the end of October or the beginning of November. Before his arrival there, however, the harmony of the congregation had been disturbed by the reception of a letter from the English residents at Zurich, who declined to come to Frankfort unless they obtained security that the Church would use the Prayer-Book of King Edward VI., on the ground that the rejection or alteration of that form of service would give occasion for the charge against them of fickleness in their religion, and would be a virtual condemnation of those who at that very time were suffering persecution on its account. To this the members of the church at Frankfort replied that they had obtained permission to use their place of worship on the condition of their conforming as closely as possible to the French ritual; that there were some things in the English book which would give offence to the Protestants of the place whose hospitality they were enjoying; that certain ceremonies in that book had been occasion of scruple to conscientious persons at home; that they were very far indeed from pronouncing condemnation of those who had drawn up that book, since they themselves had altered many things; and that the sufferers in England were testifying for more important matters than rites of mere human appointment. This answer, while it somewhat abated the confidence of the friends at Zurich, did not {86} drive them from their purpose, for they instigated their brethren at Strasburg to make the same request both by letter and by deputation, and thus widened the area of the controversy.

This was the state of things when Knox appeared upon the scene, and although his convictions were strongly on the side of those who opposed the adoption of the Book of Common Prayer, he strove to act the part of a peacemaker, as far as he consistently could. For when the congregation agreed to adopt the order of worship followed in Calvin's Church at Geneva, he declined to carry out that determination until their learned brethren in other places should be consulted. He confessed that he could not conscientiously administer the sacraments according to the English book, but he offered to restrict himself solely to the preaching of the word, and let some one else administer the sacraments; and if that freedom could not be granted to him, he desired that he might be altogether released from the pastorate to which he had been chosen. But the congregation would not consent to give him up, and in the hope of preventing future controversy, Knox, who was joined by Whittingham, afterwards Dean of Durham, and others, drew up a fair summary and description of the English Prayer-Book, which they sent to Calvin for his inspection and advice. In his reply the Genevese Reformer bewailed the existence of unseemly contentions among them; claimed that he had always counselled moderation respecting external {87} ceremonies, yet condemned the obstinacy of those who would consent to no change of old customs; declared that in the English liturgy he had found many "tolerabiles ineptias,"--tolerable fooleries,--which might be borne with in the beginning of the Reformation, but ought to be removed as soon as possible; gave it as his opinion that the circumstances of the exiles in Frankfort warranted them to attempt the removal of such blemishes; and rather caustically remarked that "he could not tell what they meant who so greatly delighted in the leavings of popish dregs."

This letter produced considerable effect, and a committee, of which Knox was one, was appointed to draw up a form which might harmonize all parties. When this committee met, Knox acknowledging that there was no hope of peace unless "one party something relented," indicated how far he was willing to go in the direction of compromise; and the result was the drawing up of a form of which "some part was taken from the English Prayer-Book, and other things put to, as the state of the Church required." By the consent of the congregation this order was to continue until the month of April; and if any contention should meanwhile arise, the matter was to be referred for decision to these five learned men, namely, Calvin, Musculus, Martyr, Bullinger, and Vyret. This agreement was put in writing, and subscribed by the members of the congregation amid the joy of all. "Thanks were given to God, brotherly reconciliation followed, great familiarity (was) used, and the former {88} grudges forgotten; yea, the Holy Communion was upon this happy agreement also ministered."

But this peace was not of long continuance, for on the 13th of March Dr. Richard Cox, who had been the preceptor of Edward VI., and who was afterwards a bishop under Queen Elizabeth, arrived in Frankfort with a company like-minded with himself; and on the very first day on which they attended public worship, they broke the concordat by indulging in audible responses. When they were expostulated with by some of the seniors, or elders, of the congregation for their disorderly conduct, they replied that "they would do as they had done in England, and that they would have the face of an English Church;" and on the following Sunday one of their number, without the knowledge or consent of the congregation, entered the pulpit and read the Litany, while the rest answered aloud. This was a still more flagrant breach of the agreement, for Knox and his friends specially objected to the Litany; and therefore on the afternoon, it being his turn to preach, Knox made a public protest against such procedure. He showed how after long trouble and contention among them, a godly agreement had been made, and how it had been ungodly broken, "which thing it became not the proudest of them all to have attempted." He further alleged that as we must seek our warrant for the establishing of religion from the word of God, and without that nothing should be thrust into any Christian congregation; and as in the English Prayer Book there {89} were, as he was prepared to prove, things both superstitious, impure, and imperfect, he would not consent that it should be received in that Church; and he declared that if the attempt should be made, he would not fail to speak against it from that place, as his text might furnish occasion. He also affirmed that, among other things which provoked God's anger against England, slackness to reform religion when time and opportunity were granted was one; and as an instance of that slackness he specified, to the sore wounding of some then present, the allowing of one man to have three, four, or five benefices, to the slander of the gospel, and the defrauding of the people.

This remonstrance brought things to a crisis, and on the following Tuesday the congregation met to take the whole matter into consideration. Cox and his company claimed the right of sitting and voting with the rest, but it was contended that they should not be admitted until they had subscribed the discipline of the Church. This objection would have prevailed, but on the intercession of Knox they were received, and they rewarded his magnanimity by outvoting him, and, at the instigation of Cox, discharging him from preaching and from all interference in the affairs of the congregation. This, however, only made matters worse; and to prevent a disgraceful tumult, the whole case was referred to the senate of the city, from whom they had obtained permission to use the place of worship in which they assembled. That body, after in vain recommending a {90} private accommodation, issued an order requiring the congregation to conform exactly to the French ritual, and threatening if that were disobeyed to shut up the church. With this injunction Cox and his party outwardly complied for the time; but seeing the influence which Knox possessed, and having no hope of carrying their point so long as he should remain among them, they took means of the basest sort to get him out of the way. For two of them went privately to the magistrates of the city and accused Knox of high treason against the emperor, and against Mary, Queen of England, putting forth as the ground of their charge those passages from the Faithful Admonition which we have already quoted. On receipt of this charge the magistrates sent for Whittingham, and asked him concerning the character of Knox, whom he described in his reply as "a learned, grave, and godly man." They then informed him of the charge which had been preferred against him, and requested that he would furnish them with an exact Latin translation of the sentences of his tract, nine in number, which had been brought to their particular attention. They gave orders also that meanwhile Knox should desist from preaching until their pleasure should be known. With this command Knox loyally complied; but when he appeared next day in the church as an ordinary hearer, not thinking that any would be offended at his presence, "some departed from the sermon, protesting with great vehemence that they would not tarry where he was."

{91}

The action of the informers was most embarrassing to the magistrates, who abhorred the malice by which they were evidently actuated, but at the same time feared that the matter might come to the ears of the emperor's council then sitting at Augsburg, and that they might be compelled to give Knox up to them or to the Queen of England; and as the best means of extricating themselves from the difficulty, they suggested that he should privately withdraw from the city. Accordingly on the evening of the 25th of March, 1555, he delivered a most consolatory address to about fifty of the members of the Church in his own lodgings; and "the next day," to borrow the words of the author of the Brief Discourse, "he was brought three or four miles on his way by some of these unto whom the night before he had made that exhortation, who, with great heaviness of heart and plenty of tears, committed him to the Lord."

The sequel is soon told. Cox, by falsely representing that the congregation was now unanimous, obtained an order from the senate for the unrestricted use of the English Prayer-Book, and then procured in the Church the abrogation of the code of discipline, and the appointment of a superintendent or bishop over the other pastors. The result was that a considerable number of the members left the city, and the remainder continued a prey to strife, which Cox and his friends did not stay to compose, for they also soon took their departure to other places. The Church was thus virtually broken {92} up; and it is not without significance that, in seeking afterwards to be excused from performing service before a crucifix in the chapel of Queen Elizabeth, Cox employed the very argument which Knox had urged without effect upon himself, for he said, "I ought to do nothing touching religion which may appear doubtful, whether it pleaseth God or not; for our religion ought to be certain, and grounded upon God's word and will."

We have gone thus fully into the "Frankfort troubles," not so much because, as McCrie says, they present in miniature a striking picture of that contentious scene which was afterwards exhibited on a larger scale in England, or because it would not be difficult to find similar divisions on precisely similar points in the days in which we live, but because of the insight which the history gives us into the character of Knox himself. The controversy was keen and bitter; but throughout it all our Reformer shows to great advantage,--evincing what Carlyle has called "a great and unexpected patience," by which we suppose he means a patience which those who know nothing more about him than the usual caricature of his character, which too many have accepted, would hardly have expected. But the readers of his letter to his Berwick friends, on which we have already commented, could have looked for nothing else at his hands; and we commend the study of this episode in his history to all those who have been accustomed to regard him as a dogmatic, domineering, impracticable {93} man, who was determined always to have his way in the scorn of every consequence. The offer to restrict himself solely to preaching, or, if that should not be granted, to go quietly away, stands out to his lasting honour, and shows how eager he was to prevent all strife; while the simple mention by the chronicler of the "plenty of tears" shed by those who accompanied him out of the city, witnesses to the tenderness of his friendship; and by both alike we are reminded of the great apostle whose words were so constantly upon his lips. In reviewing the whole case, he cannot help recalling that his opponents had brought against him the old cry, "He is not Caesar's friend;" but he prays for them thus, "O Lord God, open their hearts that they may see their wickedness, and forgive them for Thy manifold mercies; and I forgive them, O Lord, from the bottom of my heart. But that Thy message sent by my mouth should not be slandered, I am compelled to declare the cause of my departing, and so to utter their folly, to their amendment I trust, and the example of others who, in the same banishment, can have so cruel hearts to persecute their brethren." His opponents tried to excuse themselves, and in a letter to Calvin put the best possible construction on their case; but nothing said by them altered the opinion of the great Reformer, in which we are persuaded all fair-minded men, whatever may be their ecclesiastical opinions will agree, to this effect:-- "But certainly this one thing I cannot keep secret, that Mr. Knox was, in my judgment, neither godly nor {94} brotherly dealt withal." It was a hard and bitter experience, and no doubt it had its influence in determining him, when he came to deal with the Reformation of Scotland, to make more thorough work of it than they had done in England.

CHAPTER VIII.

THE MINISTRY AT GENEVA, 1555-1559.

On his departure from Frankfort Knox made his way to Geneva, whither he was followed by a considerable number of those who had adhered to him in the former city. There it seems evident that he was invited by them, and probably also by others who had joined them, to resume his pastoral labours; for at the solicitation of Calvin, the Lesser Council of Geneva granted for the joint use of the English and Italian congregations the church called the Temple de Nostre Dame la Nove; and it is recorded that on the first of November, 1555, when the English Church was formed, Christopher Goodman and Arthur Gilby were "appointed to preach the word, in the absence of John Knox." This indicates that Knox was already recognised as one of the permanent pastors of the Church, and that just at that time he was for some reason or other, away for a long season from the scene of his labours.

Where he was and what he was doing we have ample means of tracing, for in the September of that {96} year we find him back again in Scotland, for the first time since he had been taken prisoner by the French. But much as he cared for the spiritual interests of his native land, it is probable that his return to Great Britain at this time was more immediately prompted by feelings of a personal nature. We have already referred to his attachment to Marjory Bowes, daughter of Richard Bowes, and of Elizabeth Aske, of Aske, near Berwick, and Dr. Laing has given strong reasons for believing that he came now for the purpose of making her his wife. The precise date of his marriage, indeed, is uncertain. Dr. McCrie has put it in 1553, before he left England on the ground that after that date Knox invariably addressed Mrs. Bowes as his "mother" and spoke of Marjory as his "wife." The truth, however, seems to have been that owing to the strong opposition of her father and other relatives to the alliance, and also, perhaps, to the very uncertain position of the Reformer himself, in these times of unsettlement and peril, they contented themselves in 1553 with formally pledging themselves to each other "before witnesses." But now, immediately on his landing, at a point on the east shore not far from the boundary between England and Scotland, he repaired to Berwick, where he found Marjory and her mother enjoying the happiness of religious society. After this, he visited Scotland, where he laboured for some months, and the marriage may not have taken place until the time when, preparatory to their setting out for Geneva, Mrs. Bowes {97} resolved to leave all her relatives and cast in her lot with her son-in-law.

The visit of Knox to Scotland, at this juncture, was of immense service to the cause of the Reformation. The clergy, unable or unwilling to discern the signs of the times, had sunk into supineness, under the belief that what they called heresy had been well-nigh banished from the land. Arran, now Duke of Chatellerault, had given place as Regent to Mary, the mother of Mary Queen of Scots, whose policy it was just then to temporize with the Protestant nobles, and to disguise for a season her deep-rooted and undying hatred of their cause. In the good providence of God, also, a number of the leading adherents of the new faith, like Erskine of Dun, Maitland of Lethington, and others, had come to Edinburgh to confer with and enjoy the ministrations of John Willock, who had been sent over by the Duchess of East Friesland, ostensibly on a commercial mission to the Scottish court, but really to see "what good work God would do by him to his native land;" and the private meetings which he held with the Protestants in Edinburgh for prayer and the exposition of the word, may have suggested to Knox that he should follow a similar plan. That at least was the course which he determined to pursue. He was received into the houses of certain burgesses whose names he has enshrined in his history, and though the number of meetings and the necessity of holding them in secret kept him busy night and day, he was greatly {98} encouraged by the results. Writing to Mrs. Bowes, he says that "the fervent thirst of his brethren, night and day, sobbing and groaning for the bread of life, was such, that if he had not seen it with his own eyes he could not have believed it;" and again that "the fervency here did far exceed all others that he had seen;" and "did so ravish him, that he could not but accuse and condemn his slothful coldness."

The news of his arrival spread among the Reformers in all parts of the country, and his presence was so eagerly desired everywhere that he was obliged to postpone his return to Berwick, and enter upon a series of evangelistic journeys through different districts of the land. But we will allow him to describe his work at this time himself. Thus he writes in his "History": "John Knox, at the request of the Laird of Dun, followed him to his place of Dun, where he remained a month, daily exercised in doctrine, whereunto resorted the principal men of that country. After his returning, his residence was most in Calder, where repaired unto him the Lord Erskine, the Lord Lorn, and Lord James Stuart, Prior of St. Andrews (half-brother to Mary Stuart), where they heard and so approved his doctrine, that they wished it to have been public. That same winter he taught commonly in Edinburgh; and after the Yule (Christmas) by the conduct of the Laird of Barr, and Robert Campbell of Kinzeancleugh, he came to Kyle, and taught in the Barr, in the house of the Carnell, in the Kinzeancleugh, in the town of Ayr, {99} and in the houses of Ochiltree and Gadgirth, and in some of them ministered the Lord's Table. Before the Pasch (Easter) the Earl of Glencairn sent for him to his place of Finlaston, where, after doctrine, he likewise ministered the Lord's Table; whereof, besides himself, were partakers his lady, two of his sons, and certain of his friends. And so returned he to Calder, where divers from Edinburgh, and from the country about, convened as well for the doctrine as for the right use of the Lord's Table, which before they had never practised. From thence he departed the second time to the Laird of Dun, and teaching them in greater liberty, the gentlemen required that he should minister likewise unto them the Table of the Lord Jesus; whereof were partakers the most part of the gentlemen of the Mearns, who professed that they refused all society with idolatry and bound themselves to the uttermost of their power to maintain the true preaching of the Evangel of Jesus Christ, as God should offer to them preachers and opportunity." Well done, ye men of the Mearns, and ye worthy descendants of the Lollards of Kyle! Often in the history of Scotland have the dwellers in these parts stood up manfully for the truth, but never was a nobler thing done in either locality, than when ye thus received and welcomed the apostle of your country's Reformation!

Such labours were sure sooner or later to attract the attention of the bishops; and accordingly while he was in the Mearns he was summoned to appear {100} before them at Edinburgh, in the Church of the Blackfriars, on the 15th May, 1556. They probably imagined that this mere "show of force" on their part would suffice to frighten him into silence. If they did, they reckoned without their host; for encouraged by his friends he came to Edinburgh to meet and face his accusers. But when it came to the pinch, they shrank from the encounter; and so it was that on the very day on which he had been summoned to stand before them, he preached, of all places, in the very lodging of the Bishop of Dunkeld, to a greater audience than he had hitherto addressed in Edinburgh. For ten days he continued morning and afternoon at this work, and so thoroughly was his heart refreshed by it that he writes of it thus to Mrs. Bowes: "O sweet were the death that should follow such forty days in Edinburgh as here I have had three."

But the boldest, if we should not call it the most audacious thing, which he did in this visit, was to address a letter to the Queen Regent, wherein he vindicated himself from the charges made by his enemies against him, and exhorted her to hear the word of God, and regulate her government by its principles. The suggestion to send such an epistle came from the Earl Mareschal and Henry Drummond, who had been brought to hear him by Lord Glencairn, and who declared, on what they said they knew of the queen's mind, that she was in a mood to be propitious. But though the letter is correctly described by Lorimer as one "which for its {101} courtesy of phrase, and faithfulness of counsel, was equally suitable to her dignity as a queen, and to his character as a minister of God," it met with only a mocking reception. "Please you, my lord, to read a pasquil," said Mary of Guise, after it had been put into her hands, and while she was giving it to the Archbishop of Glasgow, and that was all the notice of it which she condescended to take. This treatment of his expostulation being reported to Knox, revealed to him how little he had to expect from Mary of Guise; and as just at this time letters arrived from Geneva "commanding him, in God's name, as he that was their chosen pastor, to repair unto them for their comfort," he made immediate preparations for his departure thither. He took leave of the several congregations to whom he had preached, and sent on his wife and his mother-in-law to Dieppe before him, there to await his arrival. He reached them in the month of July, and shortly after went with them to Geneva; for in the "Livre des Anglois" there is an entry to the effect that on the 13th of September, 1556, John Knox; Marjory, his wife; Elizabeth, her mother; James ----, his servant; and Patrick, his pupil, were received and admitted members of the English Church and congregation there.

The reception of Mrs. Bowes into his household, especially with his knowledge of her deep-seated melancholia, says much for the kindliness of Knox's heart; and contrasts strongly with the spirit manifested on a similar matter by that other Scotsman whose {102} correspondence has so recently been given to the world. We know not if the cheap sneer indulged in by so many at the expense of the mother-in-law were as common in his days as it is in ours, but, in any case, Knox in all this was thoughtfully tender, and though he admits that the desponding habit of Mrs. Bowes was often a great trial to him, yet he never withdrew his regard from her. The following sentences of Dr. Laing express all that needs to be said more on this subject: "Her husband, I presume, was a bigoted adherent of the Roman Catholic faith, and this may serve as the key both to his opposition to Knox's marriage with his daughter, and to the mother's attachment to her son-in-law. It cannot at least be said that Knox was actuated by the expectation of wealth. In his last will and testament he states that all the money he received from the mother's succession for the benefit of his two sons was one hundred marks sterling, which he, 'out of his poverty,' had increased to five hundred pounds Scots, and had paid through Mr. Randolph to their uncle, Mr. Robert Bowes, for their use. The comparative value of money at this time was very variable; but we may reckon (that) the hundred marks, or ?6 13s. 4d., were increased by Knox to ?00 sterling."[1]

After Knox left Scotland the courage of the bishops revived, for they actually summoned him again, and on his failure to put in an appearance they were bold enough to burn him in effigy at the Cross of Edinburgh! {103} But this brutum fulmen of theirs could not undo the work which he had wrought. For by his labours at this time, especially in exposing the evil of the Protestants' any longer countenancing, papal worship, he detached from the Romish communion the nucleus round which the Church of Scotland, in a reformed state, was ultimately to form itself. Hitherto there had been no separate organization of the adherents to the Protestant faith; and no formal observance by them of the ordinance of the Supper. But now they had, to some extent at least, committed themselves to ultimate separation from the Church of Rome. As Lorimer says, "They were now a "Congregation" or community of Evangelical Christians, as much bound to one another as they were dissevered from the Church of the popes." And Knox's leaving of them in that condition was as much for their good as his arrival among them some months before had been. Had he remained longer in Scotland at this time, his presence would have undoubtedly provoked an outburst of persecuting fury on the part of the bishops and their friends; while as it was, the seed which he sowed had opportunity to root itself in the hearts of those who had received it at his hands; and this it would assuredly do if they followed the directions which he had left behind him. For before his departure he drew up a letter of wholesome counsel addressed to his brethren in Scotland, in which he exhorts them to give themselves to the daily study of the Bible and worship of God in their homes, and gives them {104} directions as to the holding and conducting of assemblies for public worship and mutual conference and prayer, recommending them to observe a regular course in their reading, and cautioning those who should speak, to do so with modesty, avoiding "multiplication of words, perplexed interpretation, and wilfulness in reasoning." If anything occurred in the text which they could not resolve for themselves, he advised them to apply for assistance to the more learned, and offered if they should refer it to him, to give them such help as he could render, saying, "I will more gladly spend fifteen hours in communicating my judgment with you, in explaining as God pleases to open to me any place of Scripture, than half an hour in any matter beside."

To the same period belong his "Answers to some Questions concerning Baptism," etc., which had been proposed to him by some inquirers, and which are of a sort that have often troubled young converts in similar cases. They are, whether baptism administered by the popish priests was valid and did not require repetition? Whether the decree of the apostles and elders at Jerusalem be still in all its points binding on believers? Whether the prohibition in 2 John 10 extended to the common salutation of those who taught erroneous doctrine? How the directions respecting dress in 1 Peter iii. 3 are to be obeyed? and the like. And with them all he deals in a spirit of wisdom for which multitudes unacquainted with his works would hardly give him credit. We need not enter into details regarding them; {105} but as the first mentioned of the above subjects was debated a few years ago in the Assembly of the Presbyterian Church (North) of the United States, it may not be uninteresting to state that, while Knox declares unequivocally that it would be wrong for Protestant believers to seek baptism for their children from popish priests, he yet as plainly affirms that a man who had been baptized in infancy in papistry ought not to be rebaptized when he cometh to knowledge, because Christ's institution could not be utterly abolished by the malice of Satan or by the abuse of man.

From September, 1556, to September, 1557, Knox laboured in Geneva, delighting in his work and rejoicing in the fellowship of congenial friends. Indeed, these halcyon months seem to have been the most peaceful of his chequered life, and we do not wonder that he wrote regarding Geneva: "I neither fear nor shame to say, it is the most perfect school of Christ that ever was in the earth since the days of the apostles." In the public services of the Church he used the form of prayer which had been drawn up by himself and others for the English congregation, and which was the groundwork of the "Book of Common Order" that was received by the Church of Scotland in 1565. But as that will come up for description in its proper place, we need not dwell upon it here. The harmony of the Geneva Church was sweet after the controversies of Frankfort, and the intercourse of the brethren from England, who were then engaged in the preparation of that version of the {106} Scriptures which continued to be for nearly a hundred years the favourite Bible of the Puritans, must have been a constant joy.

But this happiness did not last long; for in the month of May (1557) James Syme and James Barron, two burgesses of Edinburgh, and his own very devoted friends, arrived with a letter from Glencairn, Lorn, Erskine, and Lord James Stuart, beseeching "in the name of the Lord," that he would return to his native land; and affirming that he would find all the faithful whom he had left behind him, not only glad to hear his doctrine, but also ready to jeopardise their lives and goods for the setting forward of the glory of God. The opinion of Calvin and other friends to whom he submitted this request, was that he could not refuse such a call "without declaring himself rebellious unto God and unmerciful to his country"; and no doubt his own heart had already given a similar response. Accordingly, after making all due arrangements for the leaving of his charge, and for the care of his family in his absence, he set out from Geneva in the end of September, and arrived at Dieppe on the 24th October. He was met there, however, with letters which gave him the impression that those who had invited him to return to Scotland had repented of their action in that regard; and that many of the professed adherents of the truth had drawn back and became faint-hearted in the cause. This brought him to a stand, and he determined to go no farther until his way should be more clear. He {107} immediately wrote to his correspondents, explaining how he came to be at Dieppe, upbraiding them for their fear and fickleness; admonishing them of the great importance of the enterprise to which they had committed themselves; and alleging that they ought to hazard their lives and fortunes to deliver themselves and their brethren from spiritual bondage. This letter is dated October 27th, 1557, and was followed by another of a more general tenour to his brethren in Scotland, which appears to have been written in the same place on the 1st of December.

In the expectation of receiving some definite information from Scotland, Knox lingered in Dieppe for some considerable time, and officiated as temporary preacher to a Protestant Church which had recently been formed there. But when no answer came to his appeal to his countrymen, he set his face again toward Geneva, to which, after visiting Lyons, Rochelle, and other towns, he returned in the spring of 1558.

But though he had heard nothing from Scotland, matters there had been making steady progress. There may have been just enough of wavering on the part of some to give occasion for the desponding letters which had arrested him at Dieppe, yet there had been no great reaction. For on the 3rd December, perhaps after the receipt of Knox's letter of the preceding October, there had been a conference of the leading Protestants as to what was best to be done, and as the result a Common Bond or Band--the earliest of those {108} covenants which have had so conspicuous a place in the church history of Scotland--was drawn up and subscribed by Argyle, Glencairn, Morton, Lorn, Erskine of Dun, and many others. By this "engagement" they pledged themselves in the most solemn manner "to strive in their Master's cause even unto death;" "to maintain, set forward, and establish the most blessed word of God, and His congregation;" with their "whole power, substance, and their very lives; and to labour to the utmost of their possibility, to have faithful ministers purely and truly to preach Christ's gospel, and minister His sacraments to His people."

This was brave and hopeful in the highest degree. But Knox knew nothing of it meanwhile, and in his despondency composed and issued that tract which must be pronounced the greatest mistake of his life. We refer, of course, to "The First Blast of the Trumpet against the monstrous Regiment (i.e. government) of Women," which is an elaborate argument designed to establish the proposition that "to promote a woman to bear rule, superiority, dominion, or empire, above any realm, nation, or city, is repugnant to nature, contumely to God, a thing most contrarious to His revealed will and approved ordinance; and finally it is the subversion of good order, of all equality and justice." We have already seen from the questions which he put to Bullinger, that he had been pondering this subject for some time; and there is evidence in the tract itself, that he had diligently consulted what we should now {109} call "the literature of the subject," for he refers to Aristotle's politics; to the Books of the Digests; to such Fathers of the Church as Tertullian, Augustine, Ambrose, Chrysostom, etc. But it was clearly prompted by the fact that Mary Tudor was on the throne of England; and there is throughout a strong undercurrent of application to her character and cruelties. Whatever opinion may be taken on the main question, however,--and the very existence of the Salic law in some states still proves that there are two sides to it, there can be no doubt that Knox's treatment of it at all, not to speak of the sort of treatment which he gave it, was at this time impolitic and imprudent. In his preface he intimates that he is prepared to be condemned by multitudes, and even for being accused by some of high treason; and doubtless, he thought that he had counted the cost before he built his tower. But the publication brought such a storm about his head, that though he had purposed to follow his first blast with a second and a third, the two latter were never blown. His friend and colleague, Christopher Goodman, put himself by his side in a work entitled "How Superior Powers ought to be Obeyed of their Subjects;" and at a later day John Milton, in quoting from Goodman, and referring to him and others, in his "Tenure of Kings and Magistrates" says, "These were the pastors of those saints and confessors, who, flying from the bloody persecution of Queen Mary, gathered up at length their scattered members into {110} many congregations ... These were the true Protestant divines of England, our fathers in the faith we hold."[2] But such laudations were exceptional. Foxe, the martyrologist, wrote a long and friendly letter to Knox, in which he expostulated with him on the impropriety of its publication; and even his friend John Calvin, in a letter to Cecil, felt compelled to deny all complicity with its production. Mary Tudor did not live long to resent it; but her sister Elizabeth never either forgot or forgave it; and it prejudiced the mind of Mary Stuart against him long before she looked upon his face. Not many months after its publication he was constrained to say "My first Blast hath blown from me all my friends in England," and could he have foreseen what the alliance of Elizabeth was ultimately to do for Scotland in the very climax of her Reformation agony, we may safely say that the work would neither have been written nor published.

But his excuse (valeat quantum) is not far to seek, and we cannot do better than give it in the words of Carlyle.[3] "It is written with very great vehemency; the excuse for which, so far as it may really need excuse, is to be found in the fact that it was written while the fires of Smithfield were still blazing, on best of bloody Mary, and not long after Mary of Guise had been raised to the Regency of Scotland--maleficent crowned women these two-- covering poor England and poor Scotland {111} with mere ruin and horror, in Knox's judgment, and may we not still say to a considerable extent, in that of all candid persons? The book is by no means without merit; has in it various little traits unconsciously autobiographic, and others which are illuminative and interesting. One ought to add withal, that Knox was no despiser of women, far the reverse in fact; his behaviour to good and pious women is full of respect; and his tenderness, his filial helpfulness in their suffering and infirmities (see the letters to his mother-in-law and others) are beautifully conspicuous. For the rest his poor book testifies to many high intellectual qualities in Knox, and especially to far more of learning than has ever been ascribed to him, or is anywhere traceable in his other writings."

To this time also belongs his treatise on Predestination, in answer to an anonymous writer who called his work "The Careless of Necessity." It is the most elaborate of all the Reformer's productions, and goes into the Augustinian controversy, on the side of the great ecclesiastical father, with much vigour of logic, great clearness of language, and apt and extended references to Scripture. Nowhere else, as it seems to us, does Knox indulge in such closely compacted argument, or write in such a nervous style. He is very careful to keep himself from misrepresentation, and all he states may be accepted as true; but there is another side to the shield to which he rarely refers, and which must be admitted as implicitly as that to which he has restricted {112} his attention. It is not, of course, equal to the great work of Mozley on the same subject; but they who would master the literature of the controversy cannot afford to overlook this valuable contribution to its documents.

Knox continued at Geneva until the month of January, 1559, when, in response to a request sent to him by those who had signed the "Godly Band," which was backed by letters of a more recent date, informing him of the state of things in Scotland, he left his wife and family behind him and set out for his native land. Mary, the English queen, had now gone to her account, and her sister Elizabeth had succeeded to the throne, so that the Protestant refugees on the continent could safely return to their own country, and it was, therefore, no longer necessary for him to retain his position as pastor. Before the breaking up of the congregation, however, its members met to give thanks to God, and agreed to send one of their number with letters to their brethren in Frankfort and other places, congratulating them on the happy change which had come about at home, and requesting them to forget all past unpleasantness, while they co-operated as brethren to procure such a settlement of religion in England as would be well-pleasing to all the friends of the Reformation. Having received favourable replies to these letters, they went in a body to the council of the city, and William Whittingham, in their name, expressed to the seigneurie the gratitude which they felt for the good reception given to them during {113} their exile, presenting them at the same time as a lasting memorial of their names the "Livre des Anglois," which is still preserved among the archives of Geneva, and from which we have quoted an interesting entry. They then left the city in which they had found so safe an asylum, and Knox sent letters with them to some of his former acquaintances in England, desiring that they would obtain permission for him to travel through England on his way to Scotland. Naturally enough he wished to see some of those among whom he had formerly laboured; but there is reason to believe that his principal motive in asking this favour, at this time, was that he might disclose to Cecil the existence of a plan which had been formed by the Princes of Lorraine, with which somehow he had become acquainted, and which had for its objects the setting up of the claim of Mary Stuart to the throne of England, the dethronement of Elizabeth under pretence that she was a bastard and a heretic, the union of England and Scotland under one crown, and the suppression of the Reformation in both by bringing the whole island under the virtual control of France. But the indignation of Elizabeth at his "First Blast" was such that his request was indignantly refused, and it was with difficulty that those who presented his letters escaped imprisonment. He did not learn this result of his application until his arrival in Dieppe; and even then, impressed with the importance of the information which he had to communicate, he himself wrote to Cecil, seeking to remove all difficulties, and desiring a personal {114} interview. But this overture met with no better success; and so, determined to wait no longer for that which seemed to be hopeless, he sailed from Dieppe on the 22nd of April, and arrived at Leith on the 2nd of May, 1559. From this time up till his decease, with the exception of a brief visit which he made to England, Scotland was the sole scene of his labours; and during these thirteen years the incidents of his public life became part and parcel of the history of his country.

[1] "Works," vol. vi. p. lxvi.

[2] "Knox's Works," by Laing, vol. iv. p. 359.

[3] Carlyle's Works, vol. xii. p. 137.

CHAPTER IX.

RETURN TO SCOTLAND, 1559.

The landing of Knox in Scotland was almost dramatic in its timeliness; and though we cannot here undertake to rewrite the annals of the period, we must as briefly as possible outline the situation. The Queen Regent, who had so far succeeded in her temporizing policy as even at one time to have secured the commendation of Knox, had now openly declared herself as the enemy of the Reformation; and, at that very moment, four of its preachers were under summons, at her instance, to stand trial before the justiciary court at Stirling on the 10th of May, for "administering without the consent of the ordinaries the sacrament of the altar in a manner different from that of the Catholic Church, during three several days of the late feast of Easter, in the burghs and boundaries of Dundee, Montrose, and various other places in the sheriffdoms of Forfar and Kincardine, and for convening the subjects in these places, preaching to them, seducing them to their erroneous doctrines, and exciting seditions and tumults." How things had come to this crisis it is not hard to tell. {116} At the consultation at which the "Godly Band" was adopted, the Reformers agreed besides on these two things, viz. first, that prayers and the lessons of the Old and New Testaments should be read in English, according to the Book of Common Prayer, in every parish on Sundays and festival days by the curates, or, if they refused, by such persons within the bounds as were best qualified; and second, that the Reformed preachers should teach in private houses only, until the government should allow them to do so in public. In accordance with the latter of these resolutions, the Protestant noblemen took preachers as private chaplains into their homes, kept them under their protection, and encouraged them in informal and domestic meetings to expound the word of God. This soon came to the knowledge of the bishops, and the primate, presuming on his influence with some of Argyle's friends, wrote to that earl, expostulating with him for having John Douglas under his care. Such interference provoked a very smart and stinging retort; and the archbishop, falling back on the old tactics of persecution, thought he would strike terror into the hearts of the Protestants by another execution. He found a victim in Walter Mill, a venerable old man, who, though condemned years before as a heretic by Cardinal Beaton, had escaped the stake at that time, but was now discovered and consigned to the flames, in the midst of which he expired, with these pathetic and prophetic words upon his lips, "As for me, I am four-score and two years old, and cannot live long by the {117} course of nature, but a hundred better shall arise out of the ashes of my bones. I trust in God I shall be the last to suffer death in Scotland in this cause." This horrible deed--done on the 28th August, 1558--thrilled the people into earnestness in a moment, and determined them to make open profession of their adherence to the Reformed worship, so that their ministers were emboldened to preach and administer the sacraments in public, even without the permission of the government, for which until then they had waited.

Meanwhile, in the month of July, a formal petition had been presented to the Regent by the Protestant barons, requesting her to restrain the violence of the clergy, and asking liberty of worship according to a restricted plan, to which they were willing to conform until their grievances should be examined and redressed. To this she replied after her usual plausible fashion, in such a way as to make them believe that she was friendly to their proposals. But the hollowness of her words is apparent from the fact that in the very same month she was in consultation with the archbishop of St. Andrews, as to the course which should be adopted for checking the Reformation; yet, as she needed the help of the Protestants at the meeting of the Parliament in November for the carrying of certain measures on which her heart was set, nothing was done openly by her against them until after that date. In December, however, she gave the primate such assurances of her support, that he summoned the Reformed preachers to {118} appear before him at St. Andrews on the and of February following, to answer the charges of usurping the sacred office and of disseminating heresy. This proceeding on his part stirred up the Protestant nobles, so that they informed the Regent that if the trial went on they would be present to see justice done, and she, fearing the consequences, prevailed upon the archbishop to prorogue the trial. At the same time she summoned a convention of the nobility to meet at Edinburgh on the 7th of March, and induced the archbishop to call a provincial council of the clergy to meet in the city on the first of the same month.

When the clergy met, two representations were laid before them, one from the Protestants, asking what they felt to be needed, and another from persons still attached to the Roman Catholic faith, praying for the redress of certain grievances in ecclesiastical administration; but both were treated with indifference. A secret treaty had been entered into by them with the Queen Regent, wherein they had promised to raise a large sum of money to enable her to put down all heresy, and so in the most uncompromising confidence they confirmed all the doctrines and practices of the Church, and declared that both the preachers who administered the sacraments after the Reformed manner, and those who received them at their hands should be excommunicated.

This action of theirs convinced the Reformers that nothing was to be hoped for from the clergy, and the {119} treaty to which we have referred having somehow come to their knowledge revealed to them that they had just as little to hope for from the court; so they broke off all further negotiations and left the city. But they had scarcely gone when a proclamation was made at the Market Cross, by order of the Regent, prohibiting any person from preaching or administering the sacraments without authority from the bishops; and it was because they had disregarded that injunction that Paul Methven, John Christison, William Harlow, and John Willock were now summoned to appear at Stirling on the 10th of May, before the Court of Justiciary. When, therefore, Knox arrived at Leith on the 2nd of that month, he could truly say that he had come "even in the brunt of the battle." Nor was he dismayed thereat. Rather like the war-horse of the sacred poet, he said among the trumpets Aha! and went forth rejoicing in his strength to mingle in the fray.

The next morning the announcement of his arrival to the provincial council of the clergy which was still in session in Edinburgh broke up that assembly in haste, but not before its members had despatched a messenger with the news to the Queen Regent who was then at Glasgow, and who a few days later proclaimed Knox as a rebel and an outlaw in virtue of the sentence formerly pronounced against him in his absence by the bishops. But all this counted for little with him, for after waiting only a few hours at Edinburgh, he had already gone to Dundee, where he found the Protestants of Angus and {120} neighbourhood gathered in great numbers and determined to attend their ministers to Stirling. Lest, however, they should do harm, when they only intended to do good, they determined to halt at Perth, from which place they sent forward Erskine of Dun to inform the Regent at Stirling of the peaceable object of their approach. As usual, when she heard what he had to say, she sought to gain time by temporizing. She authorized him to promise in her name that the trial should not go on, and prevailed on him to persuade them to give up their purpose. Accordingly the larger number of them returned to their homes. But when the day appointed for the trial came, the summons was called by the Regent's orders, the ministers were outlawed for non-appearance, and all persons were prohibited, under pain of being treated as rebels, from harbouring or assisting them. Erskine, finding that he had been grievously befooled, escaped from Stirling and carried the news to Perth, where on the day of his arrival Knox preached a sermon in which he denounced the idolatry of the mass, and on which consequences followed which he did not at the moment anticipate. For after his discourse had been concluded a priest "in contempt" uncovered a rich altar-piece and prepared to celebrate mass, whereupon a youth uttered an exclamation of indignation. This provoked the priest to strike him "a great blow," and he retaliated "in anger" by throwing a stone at the priest, which hit the altar and broke one of the images. This was the spark to which the people were {121} as tow, and in the course of a few minutes everything in the church that savoured of idolatry--altar, images, ornaments and the like--was thrown down and demolished. The report of this outbreak soon gathered a mob described by Knox as "not of the gentlemen, neither of them that were earnest professors, but of the rascal multitude," who finding nothing more to be done in the church rushed to the monasteries of the Black and Grey Friars and to the Charterhouse and laid them all in ruins.

This was the beginning of that demolition of Roman Catholic edifices for which Knox has been so grievously assailed. But, without entering minutely into the merits of the question, and cheerfully admitting that--owing to human imperfection--a work like that in which our Reformer was engaged could not be carried through without the doing of some things of which men in less troublous times must disapprove, we must be permitted to advance the following considerations. First, the outbreak at Perth was in a manner accidental, and was not either premeditated or instigated by Knox. Second, when the work of purifying the churches was systematically entered upon, special instructions were given to those entrusted with it to guard against any injury to the fabrics themselves; for in a document enjoining the purgation of the Cathedral of Dunkeld and subscribed by Argyle and Ruthven on the 12th August, 1560, the parties commissioned are thus addressed: "Fail not ye, but that ye take good heed that neither the desks, {122} windows, nor doors be anywise burnt or broken, either glass-work or iron-work." Third, the work of absolute destruction was reserved for the monasteries. Now we can clearly see the reason for such a distinction. The churches were the property of the people, and after being cleansed were preserved for the people's use; but the monasteries, as Burton candidly admits, were in a manner "fortresses of the enemy," and as such were demolished. Yet even for the destruction of them Knox and his brethren are not solely to be blamed; for as the historian just named has said[1]: "In the history of the invasions directed by King Henry and Somerset we have seen enough to account for large items in the ruin that overcame ecclesiastical buildings in Scotland. For Melrose, Kelso, Jedburgh, and the many other buildings torn down in these inroads, the Scots Reformers have no censure beyond that of neutrality or passiveness. The ruined edifices were not restored as they naturally would have been had the old Church remained predominant." When all these things are taken into account, it will be seen that there is very little foundation for the common outcry against Knox in this matter.

In the present instance the demolition of the monasteries by the mob in Perth seriously complicated the situation, and gave the Regent an advantage which she was not slow to improve. For in an address to the nobility in Stirling, she so employed it as to succeed in getting their assistance in advancing against Perth", with {123} an army, for the purpose of putting down what she chose to call a dangerous rebellion. The Reformers wrote to her disclaiming all such intention; but finding her inflexible, they prepared to defend themselves, and were assisted by the opportune arrival of Glencairn from Ayrshire, with 2,500 volunteers. When therefore she reached Perth she discovered that her force was greatly outnumbered by theirs, and she was obliged to accept an "appointment," by which she engaged to leave the citizens unmolested in the exercise of their religion, and they pledged themselves to return to their homes. This agreement she violated in many ways, and so finally lost the confidence and support of Argyle and Lord James Stuart, both of whom had been thus far politically on her side, but now cast in their lot whole-heartedly with the congregation. After this experience the leaders determined to take a step in advance and set up Protestant worship in those places where their own personal influence or the adherence of the people promised success, and it was resolved to begin at St. Andrews. They therefore set a day for Knox to meet them in that city, where he arrived on the 9th of July. When the archbishop learned that he intended to preach in the cathedral he sent a message to his friends to the effect that, "In case John

Knox presented himself at the preaching-place in his town and principal church, he should make him be saluted with a dozen of culverings, whereof the most part would light upon his nose." This threat somewhat daunted those by whom he was {124} accompanied, and they endeavoured to dissuade him from preaching; but the reply of the Reformer takes its place beside Luther's words on the way to Worms, for he said, "As for the fear of danger that may come to me let no man be solicitous, for my life is in the custody of Him whose glory I seek, and therefore I cannot so fear their boast or tyranny that I will cease from doing my duty, when of His mercy He offereth me the occasion. I desire the hand or weapon of no man to defend me. I only crave audience, which if it be denied me here I must seek further where I may have it." There was no resisting such a determination, and the result justified his courage, for remembering doubtless his own words years before, while a slave in the French galley, he preached on the Sunday, nor on that day alone, but also on the four next following, without seeing anything either of the archbishop or his culverings; and such was the effect of his discourses that the provost, magistrates, and inhabitants agreed to set up the Reformed worship forthwith, and proceeded at once to strip the church of its images and to pull down the monasteries.

The report of all this taken to the Queen Regent in the palace of Falkland by the archbishop, led to the affair of Cupar Muir, which Carlyle has thus described after his own manner: "Not itself a fight, but the prologue or foreshadow of all the fighting that followed. The Queen Regent and her Frenchmen had marched in triumphant humour out of Falkland, with their artillery ahead, soon after midnight, trusting to find at St. Andrews {125} the two chief lords of the congregation, the Earl of Argyle and Lord James Stuart (afterwards Regent Murray), with scarcely a hundred men about them,-- found suddenly that the hundred men, by good industry over-night, had risen to an army; and that the congregation itself, under these two lords, was here, as if by tryst, at mid-distance, skilfully posted, and ready for battle either in the way of cannon or of spear. Sudden halt of the triumphant Falklanders in consequence; and after that a multifarious manoeuvring, circling, and wheeling, now in clear light, now hidden in clouds of mist; Scots standing steadfast on their ground, and answering message-trumpets in an inflexible manner, till, after many hours, the thing had to end in an 'appointment,' truce, or offer of peace, and a retreat to Falkland of the Queen Regent and her Frenchmen, as from an enterprise unexpectedly impossible."[2]

From this place Knox accompanied the forces of the congregation to Perth, and thence to Edinburgh, where on the 7th of July the Protestants of the city chose him to be their minister, and then for the first time his voice sounded through the cathedral of St. Giles in ringing notes of trumpet power. But soon after the lords of the congregation, having been compelled to conclude a treaty with the Regent, by the terms of which they agreed to quit Edinburgh and deliver it up to her, judged it unsafe that he, being so obnoxious to her, {126} should remain there without their protection, and so, putting the less objectionable John Willock for the time into his place, they set him free for a preaching excursion through different parts of the kingdom.

How he wrought on that occasion, and where, he has himself described in one of his letters thus: "I have been in continual travel since the day of appointment (i.e. the treaty with the Regent), and notwithstanding the fevers have vexed me the space of a month, yet have I travelled through the most part of this realm, where all praise be to his blessed Majesty, men of all sorts and conditions embrace the truth. Enemies we have many, by reason of the Frenchmen who are lately arrived, of whom all parties hope golden hills and such support as we are not able to resist. We do nothing but go about Jericho, blowing with trumpets as God giveth strength, hoping victory by His laws alone. Christ Jesus is preached even in Edinburgh, and His blessed sacraments rightly ministered in all congregations where the ministry is established; and they be these, Edinburgh, St. Andrews, Dundee, Perth, Brechin, Montrose, Stirling, and Ayr. And now Christ Jesus is begun to be preached upon the south borders in Jedburgh and Kelso, so that the trumpet soundeth over all, blessed be our God."

This was written on the 2nd September, 1559, and on the 20th, his wife, having obtained through the influence of Throckmorton, the English ambassador at Paris, that permission to pass through England which had been denied to her husband, reached Scotland in safety. Her {127} mother came with her as far as Northumberland, and after remaining a short time with her friends there, took up her abode in Knox's household, and continued a member of his family, at least till the death of her daughter, though some believe that even after that she remained with him, with but a brief interval, till her own decease. Mrs. Knox was accompanied by Christopher Goodman, who had been the colleague of her husband in Geneva, and who continued to labour in Scotland, first at Ayr and afterwards at St. Andrews, until his return to England in 1565.

But the work in Scotland was too great to be successfully carried out by its own people, even if they had been united among themselves, which, unhappily, they were not. The Reformers there had to contend not only with the adherents of the papacy in their own land, but also with the power and diplomacy of France, and therefore it was of the utmost consequence that assistance from England should be secured. It was, fortunately, also quite important for England that France should be prevented from securing a permanent hold on Scotland; but it was some time before the English queen could be induced to commit herself in any way to the cause of the Scottish congregation; and many negotiations were required before that result was obtained. Neither into the details of these, nor into the particulars of the civil war, which lasted at this time in Scotland for about a year, can we enter here. They will be found at length in the pages of the historians; and it may suffice in this {128} place to say that at last, as the fruit of the mission of the younger Maitland to the English Court, Elizabeth consented to send a fleet into the Firth of Forth, and an array across the border; and that the ultimate issue was a treaty entered upon during the siege of Leith, on the 7th July, 1560, which secured that the French troops should be immediately removed from Scotland; that an amnesty should be granted to all who had been engaged in the late resistance to the Queen Regent; that the principal grievances in the civil administration should be redressed; and that a Free Parliament should be held to settle the affairs of the kingdom.

Before this turn was given to matters, and at midnight between the 10th and 11th of June, the Queen Regent, Mary of Lorraine, the mother of the Queen of Scots, had passed away from the earth, and thus the stage was as it were cleared for the important things which were so soon to be achieved. The one Mary had gone to her account; the other had not yet come from France to take personal possession of the throne of her native land, and in the interval many things otherwise--humanly speaking at least--unattainable were obtained. "The stars in their courses" were fighting for the Reformation; the providence of God was on its side, and blind indeed must the historian be who sees no indication of that fact. But because we fully recognise His hand, it is the more important that we distinctly note also the obliquities which characterized the conduct of many of the human actors in these transactions;

and it is with a {129} sense of something like mortification that we confess that even Knox did not stand the ordeal without deterioration. He was, as Laing remarks, "a chief instigator and agent" in the negotiations with England; and, for the most part, he manifested the strictest integrity. But there is one letter extant which prevents us from being able to say that he never lent his countenance to deceit. He is writing to Sir James Croft requesting that men should be sent by him to the help of the Reformers; and in answer to the objection that the league between England and France made it impossible to do that without offending France, he says,[3] "If ye list to craft with them, the sending of a thousand men to us can break no league nor point of peace contracted between you and France; for it is free for your subjects to serve in war any prince or nation for their wages; and if you fear that such excuses shall not prevail, you may declare them rebels to your realm, when ye shall be assured that they are in our company." We mention it that we may not be accused of concealing any portion of the truth concerning him. We do not extenuate it; we cannot vindicate it. We say only that it is, so far as we know, the solitary instance of the kind in the extensive correspondence of our Reformer; that it is a clear exception to the general outspoken, and in some cases even indiscreet, frankness by which he was characterized; and that, perhaps, he caught the infection from those with whom he was treating, for Froude says of Elizabeth at {130} this time, "It is certain only that on the one hand she was distinctly doing, what as distinctly she said she was not doing; and on the other, that she was holding out hopes which, if she could help it, she never meant to fulfil;"[4] and even Cecil, as the same author proves, was a master in the same kind of craft, so that his indignant reference to Knox's proposal reads to us now like an illustration of "Satan reproving sin." It was in truth, as Laing has said, "an age of dissimulation;" but Knox knew better; he was before his age in other things, and should have been above it in this.

But enough, we gladly turn from censure to praise, and wish to direct attention at this point to Knox's views concerning civil government. There was an assembly of nobles, barons, and representatives of burghs held at Edinburgh on the 21st of October, 1559, at which the propriety or lawfulness of depriving the Queen Regent of her authority (which was afterwards resolved upon) was debated; and before which John Willock and Knox were asked to give their opinion on the question. Willock alleged that the power of rulers is limited, that they might be deprived of it on valid grounds; and that the fortification of Leith, and the introduction of foreign troops into the kingdom, was a good reason why the Regent should be divested of her authority. Knox, while agreeing with what he had said, added that the assembly might safely proceed on these principles, provided only that they did not suffer the misconduct of {131} the Regent to alienate them from their allegiance to their own proper sovereigns, Francis and Mary; that they were not actuated by any private hatred of the Regent herself; and that any sentence which they should now pronounce should not preclude her re-admission to office if she afterwards acknowledged her error, and agreed to submit to the estates of the realm. These sentiments, considering the circumstances in which the Reformers were then placed, were moderate and wise. They show how very far from revolutionary Knox and his associates were; and it is no small praise to him to say that in a struggle which strained everything to the utmost, he sought to maintain law while striving after liberty, and was careful to discriminate between condemnation of the manner in which an office was filled, and repudiation of the office itself. The relation of the Reformation from popery to civil liberty is a theme which might furnish materials for a goodly volume, and space will not allow us to enlarge upon it here; but it might be well in these days if more attention were directed to the opinions of the Reformers regarding political government, and the share which these have had in laying the foundation of freedom, as it is now enjoyed in Great Britain and the United States. So far as Knox is concerned, we could have no better summary of his views on the subject than that which is given by his great biographer, from which we quote the following sentence,[5] each clause of which is amply confirmed by {132} McCrie in the learned and elaborate note which he has appended to his statement:--"He held that rulers, supreme as well as subordinate, were invested with authority for the public good; that obedience was not due to them in anything contrary to the Divine law, natural or revealed; that in every free and well-constituted government, the law of the land was superior to the will of the prince; that inferior magistrates and subjects might restrain the supreme magistrate from particular illegal acts, without throwing off their allegiance, or being guilty of rebellion; that no class of men have an original, inherent, and indefeasible right to rule over a people, independently of their will and consent; that every nation is entitled to provide and require that they shall be ruled by laws which are agreeable to the Divine law, and calculated to promote their welfare; that there is a mutual compact, tacit and implied, if not formal and explicit, between rulers and their subjects; and if the former shall flagrantly violate this, employ that power for the destruction of the commonwealth which was committed to them for its preservation and benefit, or, in one word, if they shall become habitual tyrants and notorious oppressors, that the people are absolved from allegiance, and have a right to resist them, formally to depose them from their place, and to elect others in their room." It may surprise some of our readers to discover how fully Knox in these particulars was abreast of many of the views of the most enlightened Liberals of our generation; but even Major, the principal of the {133} Glasgow University when Knox became a student, had struck out in the same direction, and in one of his works[6] has declared that "a free people first gives strength to a king, whose power depends on the whole people;" and that "a people can discard or depose a king and his children for misconduct just as it appointed him at first;" and similar sentiments might be cited from the pages of Buchanan. Major taught them in the class, and Buchanan wrote them in his works; but Knox gave them utterance, and that too with such force, that they were widely diffused among the people, so that in due season the divine-right nonsense of the Stuarts was exploded, and the beginning of a new order of things introduced.

But even in this matter, advanced as he was, Knox was not entirely above the narrowness of his age. In common with all the Reformers, and the most of the Puritans, he held that the theocracy of the Jews was the ideal state, and as a consequence, that it was the duty of the civil government to punish idolatry with death, to set up and maintain the true religion by all the means at its disposal, and to put down heresy as rebellion. {134} Neither the statesmen nor the divines of that age seem to have perceived that the true analogue to the Jewish theocracy is the spiritual Church of Christ, and so we account for the fact that they continually referred to the Old Testament as their warrant for seeking to advance what they believed to be the truth, and to put down what they considered to be error by force. They did not remember that in the Jewish state God was in no mere figurative sense, but really and absolutely the King, so that in it to fear God and to honour the king was virtually the same thing, and sin in every form was also ipso facto crime, was indeed treason, as committed against the head of the government, and so was punishable by civil pains and penalties. Forgetting or not perceiving that, the Reformers took the Jewish for the model constitution. In all the states which they sought to remodel, they lost sight of the distinction between a theocracy and an ordinary government, and confounded crime with sin, and sin with crime. More especially they made the crime of crimes to be, the resisting or not conforming to what they themselves believed to be the true religion as revealed by God, and as such they punished that with all severity. There is no instance indeed on record of Knox himself being in any way mixed up with persecution, understanding by that word merely the putting of one to death for religious practices or opinions. No such controversy can be raised over him as that which has been held regarding Calvin and the prosecution of Servetus. But they all alike held {135} that it was the duty of the government to establish and maintain, as a government, and that means by enactments enforced by penalties, the true religion; and from that persecution follows; rather let us say, in that persecution is involved. To this error, which, however, was the common opinion of their times, may be traced most of the difficulties in which they were involved in the prosecution of their work. The world has been slow to come to it, but no perfect liberty either in Church or in state is possible save through the separation of the one from the other, and the restriction of each to its own proper domain. When this shall be attained in Scotland and England, then shall be the beginning of another era, as strongly marked as that which began in the overthrow of the Papal Church three hundred years ago. The course of our narrative takes us now into parliamentary debates, and royal closets, fully as often as into assemblies of the Church, and therefore before we enter upon this section of the history, we deem it right to indicate once for all the views which we ourselves hold upon the subject. It is the province of the biographer to narrate, and he must not be held as endorsing everything which he records.

[1] "History of Scotland," vol. iii. p. 354.

[2] "An Essay on the Portraits of John Knox," pp. 139-140. "Works," vol. xii.

[3] "Works," vol. vi. p. 90.

[4] Froude's "History of England," vol. vi. p. 273.

[5] McCrie's "Works," vol. i. p. 149.

[6] "De Historia Gentis Scotorum," book iv. chap. 22. I am indebted for these citations to my late friend, Dr. J. M. Ross, whose researches into the literature of Scotland have been recently published, and whose early death is mourned

by all who knew his worth. His work on the Pre-reformation Literature of Scotland is a perfect thesaurus of precious things, and has attracted the widest attention.

CHAPTER X.

THE RECONSTRUCTION OF THE SCOTTISH CHURCH, 1560.

The meeting of Parliament, provided for in the Treaty of Leith, was opened with great ceremony on the 1st of August, 1560, and was attended by an unusually large number of members. Knox "improved" the occasion by preaching from the cathedral pulpit a series of expository sermons on the prophecies of Haggai, with special application to the circumstances of the country at the time. On his own showing he was "vehement," and as he inveighed strongly against those who had been enriched with the revenues of the Church, his words gave great offence to many. Maitland sneeringly said, "What! we must now forget ourselves and bear the barrow to build the house of God,"--words which already showed that spirit of insincerity which afterwards took him into the opposite camp. The great matter before this Parliament, after it had approved the articles of the treaty, was the settlement of religion, and as a preliminary to that the ministers were requested to draw up a summary statement of "that doctrine which they would maintain as wholesome and true, and only {137} necessary to be believed." This work was done by them in four days, at the end of which they produced the Confession which Knox has given at full length in his history. It is all but certain that he had a considerable hand in its preparation, and it has been described by the younger McCrie as "remarkably free from metaphysical distinctions and minutiae," and as "running in an easy style, and in fact reading like a good sermon in old Scotch." It is, of course, Calvinistic, but in the article on election, there is nothing of either reprobation or preterition. In that on the Lord's Supper it repudiates alike the doctrine of transubstantiation, and that of those who believe it to be "nothing else but a naked and bare sign," insisting on some mystical influence as connected with it, but yet confessing that such influence is given "neither at that only time, nor yet by the proper power of the sacraments only," so that it is exceedingly difficult to get from it a definite statement of what precisely the "grace" in the sacrament is; but that difficulty is felt, in our judgment, as seriously by those who desire to reduce to plain language the words of the Westminster standards on the same subject. In the section which treats of the authority of Scripture, there is no attempt to formulate any theory of inspiration, but simply a declaration that "in those books which of the ancients have been reputed canonical, all things necessary to be believed for the salvation of mankind are sufficiently expressed," and an affirmation that "such as allege the Scriptures to have no other authority, but that which is received from {138} the Kirk (Church) are blasphemous against God, and injurious to the true Kirk, which always heareth and obeyeth the voice of her own spouse and pastor, and taketh not on her to be mistress of the same." On the subject of the civil magistrate its words run thus: "That to kings, princes, rulers, and magistrates, we affirm that chiefly and most principally the reformation and purgation of the religion appertains; so that not only they are appointed for civil policy, but also for maintenance of the true religion, and for suppressing of idolatry and superstition, as in David, Jehoshaphat, Hezekiah, Josiah, and others highly commended for their zeal, in that case may be espied," a statement which amply confirms what we have just said regarding the position taken by the Reformers on this matter. We ought to add, however, that according to Randolph, the representative of the English Court, who was present on the occasion of the ratification of the Confession, the section on the civil magistrate had been expunged by Maitland, to whose revision, as well as that of the Lord James Stuart, it had been submitted, and by whom certain strong phrases in other parts of the document had been softened. In Knox's history we have no word of anything like that, but simply the Confession as it was actually ratified, and in that a paragraph on the civil magistrate stands with the rest. But as there is in that paragraph a good deal about the prerogatives of rulers, and the duty of obedience to them, while there is no word of the limits of allegiance to them, and the right of {139} resisting them when they violate either the laws of the realm or the dictates of conscience, on both of which points we know that Knox and his brethren held strong convictions, it is probable that at first the article contained some things on these aspects of the question, which were afterwards stricken out, by the two men whom we have named, as being likely if retained to imperil the acceptance of the document as a whole. This is only a conjecture of our own, but it is not inherently improbable, and it serves to harmonize the statement of Randolph with the appearance in Knox's history of a chapter on the civil magistrate in the Confession as adopted.

This summary of doctrine was laid before Parliament, and carefully read over article by article. Then, that no one should have a pretext for complaining of undue haste, its further consideration was adjourned to another day, the 17th of August, on which it was almost unanimously accepted, and "ratified by the three estates of the realm." This was followed on the 24th of the same month by the passing of Acts abolishing the jurisdiction of the Pope in Scotland, repealing all former statutes passed in favour of the Roman Catholic Church, and ordaining that all who said mass, or heard mass, should for the first offence be punished with confiscation of goods, for the second with banishment, and for the third with death. Thus on the very threshold of their undertaking they manifested the same intolerance from which they had themselves suffered so much.

{140}

With a view to the proper organization of the Protestant Church, the Lords of the Privy Council appointed Knox, along with five other ministers, to draw up a plan of reconstruction which in their judgment should be both agreeable to Scripture and practicable in the circumstances of the country at the time. The outcome of their labours was that scheme of Church government and order, which is known in Scottish ecclesiastical history as "The First Book of Discipline." It specifies the officers of the Church, permanent and temporary, describes the manner of their election and appointment, particularizes their duties, and gives principles for guidance as to general discipline, while it also furnishes directions as to the celebration of marriages and the conducting of funerals. At the same time it outlines with great fulness a magnificent system of national education, such as Scotland is only now beginning to realize, though for centuries it has enjoyed something of an approximation to it.

This "Book" is one of extreme interest, and is worthy of far more attention from the mass of the people in these days than it has received, or perhaps is likely to receive; but to whet the appetites of our readers for the enjoyment of the work itself, we shall give some general notion of its contents. The permanent officers in the Church were ministers, elders, and deacons. The ministers were to be elected by the people, but in case they neglected to do that duty within forty days the Church of the superintendent with his council was to {141} "present" to them a man whom they judged apt to feed the flock, yet it was always to be avoided "that any man be violently intruded or thrust in upon any congregation." Thus Knox and his brethren were "nonintrusionists;" yet we doubt if in the famous controversy which ended in 1843, they would have come up to the party standard, for the "Book" says: "But violent intrusion we call not, when the council of the Kirk, in the fear of God, and for the salvation of the people, offereth unto them a sufficient man to instruct them, whom they shall not be forced to admit before examination." Then elsewhere it is said, "If his doctrine is wholesome and able to instruct the simple, and if the Kirk can justly reprehend nothing in his life, doctrine, or utterance, then we judge the Kirk which before was destitute unreasonable if they refuse him whom the Kirk did offer, and they should be compelled by the censure of the council and Kirk, to receive the person appointed and approved by the judgment of the godly and learned." Where was "the veto without reasons" then? And on whose side was the First Book of Discipline? or was it on both sides? The minister so chosen or appointed was to give proof of his gifts by interpreting before the men of soundest judgment in the neighbourhood, some place of Scripture selected by his brethren in office. He was also to be examined openly "before all that list to hear," by the ministers and elders of the Kirk, "in all the chief points that now lie in controversy betwixt us and the Papists, {142} Anabaptists, Arians, or other such enemies of the Christian religion." Next he was to preach to the congregation calling him, that in open audience of his flock he might give confession of his faith in full. Then public "edict" was to be proclaimed, not only in the church where he was to serve, but also in other places, especially in those in which he had formerly lived, that if there was known any reason why he should not be appointed to the ministry it should be shown. If everything were satisfactory, the manner of his installation to office was to consist in the consent of the people to whom he was appointed and the approbation of the learned ministers by whom he was examined. The admission was to be "in open audience." After a sermon by some "especial minister" on the duty and office of ministers, exhortations were to be given to minister and people, and this paragraph follows: "Other ceremony than the public approbation of the people and declaration of the chief minister, that the person there presented is appointed to serve that Kirk, we cannot approve; for albeit the apostles used the imposition of hands, yet seeing the miracle is ceased, the using of the ceremony we judge is not necessary." Most evidently John Knox believed in "order," but just as evidently he did not believe in "orders," and there is no place here for the doctrine of "succession."

The elders and deacons were to be chosen by the people annually, from among a list given by the minister, and if Churches be of smaller number than that such {143} office-bearers can be chosen from among them, they may be joined to the next adjacent Church. We have here therefore the "rotatory" eldership, as it has been called by some in America, recognised in principle, and the reason given for it is "lest that by long continuance of such officials men presume upon the liberty of the Church." Those holding the office were eligible for re-election, but they must be appointed yearly "by common and free election." In another place he says: "This order has been ever observed since that time in the Kirk of Edinburgh, that is that the old session before their departure nominate twenty-four in election for elders, of whom twelve are to be chosen, and thirty-two for deacons, of whom sixteen are to be elected, which persons are publicly proclaimed in the audience of the whole Kirk, upon a Sunday before noon, after sermon, with admonition to the Kirk, that if any man know any notorious crime or cause that might unfit any of these persons to enter in such vocation they should notify the same unto the session the next Thursday; or if any know any persons more able for that charge, they should notify the same unto the session, to the end that no man, either present or absent, being one of the Kirk, should complain that he was spoiled of his liberty in election." The duty of the elders was to assist the minister in the oversight and discipline of the flock; and that of the deacons was to superintend the revenues of the Church and to take care of the poor.

Besides these permanent offices, two others were {144} recommended for the meeting of present emergencies. There were first a class of men called Readers, whose duty it was to read the Common Prayers and the Scriptures, in places still destitute of properly qualified ministers, and which otherwise would have had no service of any sort for public worship or instruction. They were restricted to the function of reading, and hence their name; but they were encouraged to prosecute their studies, and if they advanced satisfactorily they were permitted, after examination, to append some exhortations to their readings, and then they were called Exhorters. In addition to these, and at the other end of the scale, the Book recommended the appointment of ten Superintendents, each of whom was to have the supervision of a district over which he was required regularly to travel for the purpose of preaching, planting Churches, and inspecting the conduct of ministers, exhorters, and readers. Some have maintained that in this there was a recognition of Episcopacy, but as Dr. Laing has shown, the office was merely temporary, and the number never exceeded the five who were first appointed. Like other ministers the superintendent was subject to the Assembly, and might be censured, superseded, or deprived of his office by its decision. These office-bearers were to be appointed in the first instance by the Privy Council, or by a commission appointed by that body for the purpose; but, afterwards, by the whole ministers of the district to be superintended, from a list of names already proclaimed by the ministers, elders, {145} and deacons with the magistrates and council of the chief town in the province; and for his installation a form is given, with a list of the questions to be proposed to him, and the answers to be given by him. It is added that "the superintendent being elected and appointed to his charge, must be subjected to the censure and correction of the ministers and elders, not only of his chief town, but also of the whole province over the which he is appointed overseer."

It may be added here, that "The Book of Common Order" makes mention of still another class of office-bearers, called Teachers or Doctors, who were to be men of learning for the exposition of God's word, and whose nearest modern equivalent seems to us to be the professors in theological seminaries, but it is said "for lack of opportunity we cannot well have the use thereof."

In regard to the sacraments the "Book of Discipline" lays down that the Lord's Supper should be observed after the manner already described by us when we were treating of Knox's ministry in Berwick. In great towns it was recommended that it should be observed four times in the year, and in order to keep off Easter, the first Sundays in March, June, September, and December are suggested, because "we study to suppress superstition." It was also specified that in large towns there should be daily sermon, or else common prayer, with some exercise of reading the Scriptures; and in smaller places there should be at least one day besides the {146} Sunday appointed for sermon and prayer. Baptism might be administered wherever the word was preached, but it is alleged to be more expedient that it be on the Sunday, and never in private unless accompanied by the preaching of the word; for as the Book of Common Order says, "The sacraments are not ordained of God to be used in private corners as charms or sorceries, but left to the congregation and necessarily annexed to God's word as seals of the same." We admit the clause about "charms," but with the household baptisms of the Scriptures before us, and the other baptisms, which were administered--as it were "extempore"--by the apostles in the house of the jailer and the house of

Cornelius, we are not quite so sure about the rest of "the rubric." Marriages were not to be entered into secretly, but in open face and audience of the church; the place for their celebration, therefore, was the church, and the time recommended was Sunday before sermon. It was suggested that there should be no service of any sort at funerals; but it is added, "Yet we are not so precise but that we are content that particular kirks use services in that behalf, with the consent of the ministry of the same, as they shall answer to God, and to the assembly of the Church gathered within the realm."

But the most interesting portion of the Book of Discipline, perhaps, to us in these days, is that which refers to education, contemplating as it did the erection of a school in every parish for the instruction of the {147} young in the grammar of their own language, in the Latin tongue, and in the principles of religion; the setting up in every notable town of a "college" for the teaching of "the arts, at least, logic and rhetoric, and the tongues;" and finally the establishment in the "towns accustomed,"--that is Aberdeen, St. Andrews, and Glasgow,--of Universities with full appointments which are minutely described. These were to be supported, stipends were to be furnished for the superintendents, ministers, and readers, and suitable provision made for ministers' widows, and orphan children, out of the confiscated revenues of the Church, the bishops, and the cathedral establishments, together with the rents arising from the endowments of monasteries and other religious foundations.

The "Common Prayer" so frequently referred to was no doubt "the order of Geneva which is now used in some of our kirks," as the words within inverted commas quoted from the Book of Discipline make clear. That book had been prepared for the English congregation of Geneva during Knox's pastorate there; and with such changes as the difference of circumstances made necessary, it came to be adopted by the Scottish General Assembly in 1564. Our reference to it here, therefore, is a little premature, as we are now writing of events that occurred in 1560; but it may be convenient, as we are treating of the organization of the Scottish Church, to dispose of the matter, once for all, in this place. As we have already incidentally {148} recorded, it was agreed by those who entered into the "Godly Band," that "common prayers" be read in the parish churches on Sundays by the curates if they consented, or if they refused, by such persons within the bounds as were best qualified to do so. This probably was meant to specify the second Prayer-

Book of King Edward VI., yet as Dr. Laing remarks, and the reasoning of Dr. McCrie on the subject tends to confirm his statement, "the adoption of that book could only have been to a partial extent, and of no long continuance." He proceeds thus: "But this, after all, is a question of very little importance, although it has been keenly disputed, for it is well to remember that at this period there were no settled parish churches, and as there were no special congregations either in Edinburgh or in any of the principal towns throughout the country, no ministers had been appointed. The lords of the congregation and their adherents were much too seriously concerned in defending themselves from the Queen Regent and her French auxiliaries, and more intent for that purpose on obtaining the necessary aid from England, than to be at all concerned about points of ritual importance. In the following year, when the French troops were expelled from Scotland, and the Protestant cause was ultimately triumphant, we may conjecture that, in some measure swayed by the avowed dislike of Knox to the English service book, the preference was given to the forms of Geneva. We hear at least no more word of the English Prayer-Book, and {149} in the "Book of Discipline," prepared in December, 1560, the only form mentioned is "Our Book of Common Order," and "The Book of our Common Order, called the Order of Geneva." There is also in existence a copy of an edition of that book printed in Edinburgh in 1562, which shows its actual use at that time. Afterwards it was found needful to have it enlarged, and the metrical version of the Psalms, taken in large proportion from Sternhold and Hopkins, and accompanied with appropriate tunes, was appended to it. We cannot go into all the details of each part of the service here, but will content ourselves with giving the order which it follows. It begins with a confession of faith of considerable extent, but following the lines of the Apostles' Creed of which it is an expansion; then come sections in the order in which we name them, and respectively entitled--Of the Ministers and their Election, Of the Elders and as Touching their Office and Election; Of the Weekly Assembly of the Ministers, Elders and Deacons; Of the Interpretation of the Scriptures. After these comes the sanctuary service proper, consisting first of a prayer of confession, of which a choice of one or other of three forms is given, or perhaps it may have been intended that all three should be used, for the book is not so explicit here as elsewhere; second, a psalm to a plain tune sung by the people; third, a prayer by the minister for the assistance of God's Holy Spirit, for which no form is given, and the minister is to offer it as the Holy Spirit shall move his heart; fourth, the {150} sermon; fifth, a prayer for the whole state of Christ's Church, and for the Queen and her council, and the whole body of the commonwealth; sixth, the Apostles' Creed; seventh, a psalm sung by the people; eighth, the Benediction, after one or other of two forms, to wit, that of Aaron and his sons, or that of the apostle at the end of the first Epistle to the Corinthians, but in both instances "us" is substituted for "you;" and so the congregation departeth. To this are appended the Genevan form of prayer after sermon; and another form to be used after sermon, on the week-day appointed for common prayer; prayers used in the churches of Scotland during the time of their persecution by the French; the thanksgiving after their departure; and a prayer for the general assemblies of the Church. It will be observed that nothing is here said of the reading of the Scriptures, but this was not because that was under-valued, but because the reader, who was in many cases the minister's assistant, had already, before the commencement of the service proper, attended to that duty in the hearing of the people. So far were Knox and his friends from slurring over that exercise, that in the Book of Discipline this characteristic passage occurs: "Further, we think it a thing most expedient and necessary that every church have a Bible in English, and that the people be commanded to convene to hear the plain reading or interpretation of the Scriptures as the Church shall appoint, that by frequent reading this gross ignorance, which in the {151} accursed papistry hath overflown all, may partly be removed. We think it most expedient that the Scriptures be read in order, that is, that some one book of the Old and the New Testament be begun and orderly read to the end. And the same we judge of preaching, where the minister for the most part remaineth in one place; for this skipping and divagation from place to place, be it in reading, be it in preaching, we judge not so profitable to edify the Church, as the continual following of one text."

The order for baptism follows: the father, or in his absence the godfather, is to rehearse the articles of his faith (this mention of the godfather is interesting, and some may be surprised to learn, that at the baptisms in Geneva of Knox's two sons, who were born there, Whittingham was godfather to the one and Miles Coverdale to the other); the minister follows with an exposition of the Creed; after that comes a prayer; then the minister taketh water in his hand, layeth it on the child's forehead, repeating the words of the formula of baptism, and closes with an offering of thanks. The Book of Discipline had already disallowed the sign of the cross, all anointings, and the like. This is followed by "the manner of the Lord's Supper," into which we need not go, as that has been already described. Then there is a single sentence on burial, discouraging services at the grave; but after burial "the minister, if he be present and required, goeth to the church if it be not far off, and maketh some comfortable exhortation to the {152} people touching death and resurrection." The book concludes with "The Order of Ecclesiastical Discipline," pointing out the three causes of discipline--the two kinds of discipline private and public, and the like. There is in it no form for marriage; but that could be supplied from the "Order of Geneva," which in this respect follows the lines of other ecclesiastical books.

This "Book of Common Order" has often been called "John Knox's Liturgy," and within due limitations it is not inaccurately so denominated; but the term is apt to be misleading, and it needs to be added that the forms contained in it are not prescribed for constant and exclusive use, but are given more in the way of a directory to ministers as to the conduct of the service. The "Readers" of course were restricted to them; but ministers were left free to use them or not at their discretion. Thus we find in what we may call the "rubrics" such expressions as these: "When the congregation is assembled at the hour appointed, the minister useth one of these two confessions, or like in effect;" "the minister after the sermon useth this prayer following, or such like." Similar liberty is given as to the prayers in the forms for baptism and the Lord's Supper; and at the end of the form for the service on the Sunday we have this general statement: "It shall not be necessary for the minister daily to repeat all these things before mentioned; but beginning with some manner of confession, to proceed to the sermon, which ended, he useth either the prayer for all estates before mentioned, or else {153} prayeth as the Spirit of God shall move his heart, framing the same according to the time and manner which he hath entreated of." Thus the position of the book, as concerns the debate between liturgy proper and free prayer, is one of liberty, furnishing forms to those who wished to use them, and leaving those who did not to pray as the Spirit moved them; but showing to both alike what order was to be observed in the service as a whole, what subjects were to be introduced into the prayers, and in what order and connection they were to be brought into them. It ought to be noted also that this book gave a great impulse to congregational singing of psalms, which was adopted instead of that of choral anthems; and the fashion now so universal, of printing the tunes in connection with the Psalms, was followed, if not indeed introduced, so far as Scotland is concerned by it. But though Knox had undoubtedly a hand in the preparation and sanction of this so-called Liturgy, Dr. Laing has unqualifiedly affirmed "that in no instance do we find himself using set forms of prayer." The importance of the subject in itself, and the general interest now felt in it by most of the Presbyterian and Congregational Churches alike in Great Britain and America, must be our apology for going so fully into this interesting history, and for setting, as far as we may, the exact truth about it before the reader.

But we must now resume the thread of our narrative. The Book of Discipline never was so ratified as to become the law of the land. Its general outlines, {154} indeed, were followed in the organization of the Church; but though it received the signatures of many members of the Privy Council, it was bitterly opposed by others--by some because they were unwilling to disgorge the share of the Church's patrimony of which they had taken possession, and by others because of their aversion to the strict moral surveillance to which it would have subjected them. Knox puts the matter in a nutshell when he says: "Everything that impugned to their corrupt affections was called in their mockage a 'devout imagination.' The cause we have already declared: some were licentious; some had greedily gripped to the possessions of the Kirk; and others thought that they would not lack their part of Christ's coat, and that before ever He was hanged, as by the preachers they were oft rebuked." The final arrangement of the temporalities was made later, when the ecclesiastical revenues were divided into three parts, two of which were given to the ejected popish clergy for their lives; and the other was divided between the court and the Protestant ministers.

As to the conduct of public worship the General Assembly of the Church passed an Act in December, 1562, which enacted that "one uniform order shall be taken in the administration of the sacraments, solemnization of marriages, and burial of the dead, according to the Book of Geneva"; and in December, 1564, it was ordained by the same body "that minister, exhorter, and reader shall have one of the psalm books lately printed in Edinburgh and use the order contained {155} therein, in prayers, marriage, and ministration of the sacraments."

In the latter part of 1560 Knox entered upon his ministry in Edinburgh, with the Cathedral of St. Giles as his parish church, and John Cairns as his assistant or reader. The city council provided for his lodging a house at the Netherbow

Port, which had been that of the Abbot of Dunfermline, and which is now the property of the Free Church of Scotland, by whom it is preserved as a memorial of the Reformer. The council assigned him at first a stipend of ?00, besides discharging his house rent. After the settlement by the Privy Council above alluded to, he received at least a part of his stipend from the common fund of the ministers--for there was an "equal dividend" of the portion given to the Protestant clergy--and the city council added to that what was necessary to bring it up to the sum originally given. An interesting illustration of their care for his comfort is furnished in the Act of council of date 30th October, 1561, which runs thus: "The same day the provost, bailies, and council ordains the Dean of Guild with all diligence to make a warm study of deals to the minister John Knox, within his house above the hall of the same, with light and windows thereunto, and all other necessaries." But before that time a dark shadow had fallen upon his dwelling, for toward the end of December, 1560, his wife died, leaving him with his two boys to mourn her loss.

Public affairs just then also had a threatening aspect. {156} Mary and her husband, the King of France, persistently refused either to ratify the Treaty of Leith, or to confirm the settlement of the Reformed Church, and were preparing a French army for the invasion of Scotland; while agents of the Roman Catholic Church were sent over to rally the adherents of the old faith. But "man proposes and God disposes," for before the projected invasion could be carried out Francis II. died (on December 5th, 1560), and Lord James Stuart was sent by a convention of the nobility to France, not, as some have alleged, to invite Mary to Scotland, but as Lord James himself wrote to Cecil, "for declaration of our duty and devotion to her highness." Before his departure he was--we quote from Knox's "History"'--"plainly premonished that if ever he condescended that she should have mass publicly or privately said within the realm of Scotland, that then betrayed he the cause of God, and exposed the religion even to the uttermost danger that he could do. That she should have mass publicly, he affirmed that he never should consent, but to have it secretly in her chamber, who could stop her? The danger was shown, and so he departed." He left Edinburgh on the 18th of March, and on the 19th of August, 1561, Mary arrived in Scotland, where she was received with every demonstration of enthusiastic welcome.

{157}

CHAPTER XI.

KNOX AND QUEEN MARY STUART, 1561-1563.

Beautiful in person, attractive in manner, able, acute, brilliant even, in intellect, Mary Stuart had many qualities which might have been turned to good account for the welfare of her country. But, brought up in a French court, her moral code was neither of the highest nor the purest; educated under the supervision of her uncles of Lorraine, she was taught to believe that the one great object of her life was to advance the interests of the Roman Catholic Church; and sister-in-law to him whose name is for ever blackened by the massacre of St. Bartholomew, she was not likely to be over scrupulous as to the means which she would employ to gain her end. So far as she had shaped a policy to herself, when she came to Scotland, it would seem to have been to temporize with the Protestants, until she had time either to fascinate them by the spell of her personal magnetism or to crush them by her power; then to make the throne of Scotland a stepping-stone to that of England, to which she claimed to be the lawful heir, and so to bring that realm also back {158} to its allegiance to the Pope. This made her and Elizabeth implacable enemies. They were neighbours; they were cousins; they were queens, these two, and the struggle between them was to the death. One or other must go down. Each played a deep and deceitful game, but Elizabeth was moved by ambition for herself, while Mary was devoted to a cause, and so it is that as she lays her head upon the block at Fotheringay it is encircled with the halo of a kind of martyrdom, and the eye of the sternest judge is for the moment blinded to the guilt of her life by the tear of pity which dims it as he looks upon the manner of its close.

Knox and she from the very first seem to have singled each other out for a conflict hand to hand. He saw that everything which he counted dear depended on the manner in which she was dealt with; and she perceived that he was the moving spirit in that religious revolt which it was her mission to put down. He feared the effect of her blandishments upon others, and she recognised the magnitude of his influence upon the people. He saw that if she could be baffled in her efforts to re-establish popery in the land, the victory would be finally won; and she felt that so long as he had the opportunity of swaying the multitude by the fervour of his eloquence, there was no hope of gaining the end on which her heart was fixed. He was afraid of the effect of what his friend Campbell of Kingzeancleugh called "the sprinkling of the holy water of the court" upon the less reliable of his adherents; and she feared the fervour of {159} his prayers to God, and the power of his appeals to his fellow-men. So there came to be for some time a kind of duel between them, and the issue was at last a victory for Knox. We need not approve unqualifiedly of everything which he did or said in the course of the struggle, yet we must rejoice in the result, for Knox "builded better than he knew," and secured, not immediately but ultimately, the triumph of a larger liberty than that which he at the time believed in; while she was the representative of absolute power, and of a feudalism which looked upon the common people as existing for her convenience and aggrandisement rather than upon herself as the servant of the state. "What are you in this commonwealth?" was her haughty question to him on one occasion. "A subject born within the same," was his ever-memorable answer, and the outcome of it has been that now in the land he loved the sovereign is for the subjects, and not the subjects for the sovereign; it is a little difference verbally, but in reality the gulf between the two is that which divides freedom from slavery.

The first collision between them occurred a few days after her landing. Naturally enough, as some may think, she gave orders for the celebration of a solemn mass in the chapel of Holyrood on the first Sabbath after her arrival. She knew of the law passed by the Parliament in 1560; she had probably heard from Lord James Stuart the warning which had been given to him when he went to France, and therefore this act on her {160} part was a virtual throwing down of the gauge of battle at the feet of the Protestants. And thus they themselves interpreted it. Some may imagine that they attached undue importance to it; yet as Protestantism is still insisted on as a sine qu?non to succession to the British throne, those who approve the continuance of the Revolution settlement cannot consistently condemn them. Moreover, it is not to be forgotten that to the Reformers the mass was more than even an idolatrous service. It was a sign of many other things: thumbscrews, racks, galley chains, gibbets and the like, which were inseparably connected with papal supremacy, and in truth, as one has said, "A man sent to row in French galleys and such like for teaching the truth in his own land, cannot always be in the mildest humour." When therefore her purpose became known, great excitement was created among the Protestants, and some spoke of preventing her by force from carrying it out; but Knox used his influence in private, against such a proposal. On the following Sunday, however, from his pulpit he showed his sense of the gravity of the crisis, when, after exposing the idolatry that was in the mass, he alleged that "one mass was more fearful unto him than if ten thousand armed enemies were landed in any part of our realm of purpose to suppress the whole religion." Hearing of this outburst Mary sent for him to the palace, whether of her own motive or at the suggestion of others is not known, and he had then, in the presence of Lord James Stuart, the first of {161} those interviews which have been so harped upon by his vituperators. We must refer our readers for the details to Knox's own account in his "History," which has been little more than simply modernised by McCrie, and must content ourselves with a mere summary of what occurred. She began by attacking him for the writing of the "First Blast," and after he had vindicated himself as best he could for that, she charged him with having taught the people to receive a religion different from that which was allowed by their princes. This brought out his views as to the limits of obedience to civil rulers, and on her interpreting his words to mean that her subjects should obey him and not her, he vehemently repudiated that misapprehension, and alleged that both rulers and subjects should obey God, and that kings should be foster-fathers, and queens nursing-mothers to His Church. That elicited the question from her which is the Church of God? and for answer thereto he referred her to the Scriptures. This in its turn raised the inquiry whose interpretation of Scripture was to be accepted? which he answered by laying down the duty of private judgment and of the comparing of one part of Scripture with another. At length she very humbly remarked that she was not able to contend with him, but that if she had those present with her whom she had heard they could answer him, and he expressed his readiness to meet before her in argument "the learnedest papist in Europe." To this she somewhat tartly retorted, "You may perchance get that sooner {162} than you believe," and he replied a little sarcastically to the effect that if he ever got it, then indeed it would be sooner than he believed. He took his leave in this courtly yet scriptural fashion, "Madame, I pray God that you may be as blessed within the commonwealth of Scotland as ever Deborah was in the commonwealth of Israel."

Thus for the first time they measured their strength, and the result was, in common speech, a draw. Mary found that Knox was made of more unyielding stuff than those whom heretofore she had been in the habit of meeting; and John formed an estimate of Mary's ability which his subsequent experience only served to confirm. It was to be no child's play between them. He could not afford to give so subtle and ready an adversary the least advantage. Writing to Cecil after this interview he says, "The Queen neither is, neither shall be of our opinion, and in very deed her whole proceedings do declare that the cardinal's lessons are so deeply printed in her heart that the substance and the quality are like to perish together. I would be glad to be deceived, but I fear I shall not. In communication with her I espied such craft as I have not found in such age."

Matters went on after this with tolerable quietness for months, and Knox kept up his stated labours as the minister of Edinburgh. What these were seem now to be surprising. He preached twice every Sunday, and thrice besides during the week on other days. He met regularly once a week with his elders for the oversight of {163} the flock; and attended weekly the assembly of the ministers, for what was called "the exercise on the Scriptures." These stated and constant labours, with the addition of frequent journeyings by appointment of the General Assembly to perform in distant parts of the country very much the duty of a superintendent for the time, were exceedingly exhausting; and the city council, wishing to relieve him of some of his duties, came (in April, 1562) to a resolution to call the minister of the Canongate to undertake the half of his charge; but their object was not accomplished till June of the following year, when John Craig became his colleague.

Meanwhile the Reformer came again into collision with the court. In the beginning of March, 1562, the Duke of Guise and the Cardinal Lorraine made that assault on a peaceable and defenceless congregation of Huguenots, which is known in French history as the Massacre of Vassy; and when the report of that was received by Mary, she was so delighted that she gave in honour of the occasion a splendid ball in the palace to her foreign servants, by whom dancing was kept up to a very late hour. This act of hers was exceedingly painful to Knox, for he had many warm friends among the Protestants of France, and his heart was saddened by the tidings of the treatment to which they had been subjected. Accordingly he gave vent to his feelings in his pulpit on the following Sunday, when he preached from the text, "Be wise now, ye kings; be instructed, ye judges of the earth." After discoursing on the dignity {164} of magistrates and the obedience which was due to them, he lamented and condemned the vices to which they were too commonly addicted, and made some severe strictures on their conduct, affirming, among other things, "that they were more exercised in fiddling and flinging, than in reading or hearing God's word," and that "fiddlers and flatterers" (John was evidently fond of alliteration) "were more precious in their eyes than men of wisdom and gravity." The report of his discourse was carried by some one to Mary; and though he had made no direct assault upon her, he was summoned on the next day to the palace. Introduced to a chamber in which she sat, surrounded by her maids of honour and principal courtiers, he was treated to a long "harangue," as he calls it (but it was no doubt a proper scolding), on the enormity of his conduct. Very wisely he heard that out without interruption; then, when his "innings" came, he complained that he had evidently been misreported to her, and craved leave to repeat to her precisely what he had said, thus adroitly contriving that for that time at least she should listen to a sermon. Beginning with the text, he went over the main points of his discourse, which, among other things, had in it this piece of sound sense: "And of dancing, madame, I said that albeit in Scripture I find no praise of it, and in profane writers that it is termed the gesture rather of those that are mad and in frenzy than of sober men; yet do I not utterly condemn it, providing that two vices be avoided: the former, that the principal {165} vocation of those that use that exercise be not neglected for the pleasure of dancing; and the second, that they dance not as the Philistines their fathers, for the pleasure they take in the displeasure of God's people." The accuracy of his rehearsal of his sermon having been confirmed by those who had heard it when it was originally given, the Queen said it was bad enough, but admitted that it had not been so reported to her; and then very naively asked, that if he heard anything of her that "misliked" him, he would come to herself and speak of it to her privately. But Knox believed that publicity was one great means of securing the vigilance, and through that the safety, of the people, and therefore he declined to accede to her request, on the ostensible ground that with the multiplicity of his labours he had not the time for running about the court and his congregation individually to deal with them for what he saw amiss. On this occasion Knox was the champion of "free speech," and "scored" a victory, so that he departed "with a reasonable merry countenance;" and when some of the bystanders said, "He is not afraid," he made reply, "Why should the pleasing face of a gentle woman affray me? I have looked on the faces of many angry men, and yet have not been afraid above measure," and so he left the Queen and the court for that time.

The Romanists, encouraged by the hope of success, began now to put forth strenuous exertions, both military and controversial, to recover their lost ground; but the {166} rising of the Earl of Huntly in the north was put down by the vigour of Lord James Stuart, who was now known as the Earl of Murray; and the success of the abbot of Crossraguel, in debate with Knox, was not such as to encourage others to follow in his footsteps. That dignitary, in his chapel in Kirkoswald, had, on August 30th, 1562, read a series of articles on the mass and kindred subjects, which he offered to defend against all comers; and on the following Sunday Knox, who happened to be in the neighbourhood and heard of the challenge, came to the church to meet him. But though he had courteously intimated to the abbot that he would be present, that dignitary did not put in an appearance, and Knox himself preached in the chapel. At the close of the service a letter from the abbot was put into his hand; and, after negotiations, they met on the 28th of September in the house of the provost of Maybole, where forty persons on each side were admitted as witnesses. The debate lasted for three days, and strangely enough was made by the abbot to turn mainly on the significance of the act of Melchizedek in bringing forth bread and wine when he went out to meet Abraham returning from his victories over the five kings, which Knox averred "appertained nothing to the purpose." At the end of the third day Knox, on the ground of the scanty accommodation at Maybole, proposed that they should adjourn to Ayr to finish the discussion; but this was declined by the abbot, who promised to come to Edinburgh and resume it there if the Queen would permit. {167} But he never came to the metropolis, though Knox alleges that he himself had applied to the Privy Council for the necessary permission. As usual in such cases, the victory was claimed for each by his own partisans; but to counteract the false reports that were circulated, Knox prepared and published the curious tract, purporting to be an accurate account of the debate, which Dr. Laing has reprinted in the sixth volume of the Reformer's works; and though the discussion itself was on an entirely irrelevant issue, Knox dealt with the very heart of the question in the prologue of his pamphlet, which is written in his most vigorous and trenchant style. One extract will show how sarcastic he could sometimes be, and with what grim humour he could occasionally treat even the most sacred subjects.

He has been comparing the making of the "wafer-god" to that of the idols so witheringly described by Isaiah in the 40th and 41st chapters of his prophecies, and then proceeds as follows: "These are the artificers and workmen that travail in making of this god, I think as many in number as the prophet reciteth to have travailed in making of the idols; and if the power of both shall be compared, I think they shall be found in all things equal, except that the god of bread is subject unto more dangers than were the idols of the Gentiles. Men made them: men make it. They were deaf and dumb: it cannot speak, hear, or see. Briefly, in infirmity they wholly agree, except that (as I have said) the poor god of bread is most miserable of all other idols; for according to their {168} matter whereof they are made, they will remain without corruption for many years; but within one year that god will putrefy, and then he must be burned. They can abide the vehemency of the wind, frost, rain, or snow; but the wind will blow that god to sea, the rain or the snow will make it dough again; yea, which is most of all to be feared, that god is a prey (if he be not well kept) to rats and mice; for they will desire no better dinner than white round gods enow. But, oh then, what becometh of Christ's natural body? By miracle it flies to heaven again, if the papists teach truly; for how soon soever the mouse takes hold, so soon flieth Christ away, and letteth her gnaw the bread. A bold and puissant mouse! but a feeble and miserable god! Yet would I ask a question: 'Whether hath the priest or the mouse greater power?' By his words it is made a god; by her teeth it ceaseth to be a god: let them advise and answer." Truly there is a ring of honest old Hugh Latimer in all this; and if there were many such passages in Knox's sermons, it is not difficult to explain how it was that "the common people heard him gladly."

In the May of the following year (1563), Knox was sent for by Mary to Loch Leven, where she was at the time residing, and treated to another "interview," in which she endeavoured to induce him to use his influence to put a stop to the prosecution of certain parties for their celebration or countenancing of the mass. But nothing of importance resulted, though from his own showing it is apparent that on this occasion he was very {169} nearly thrown off his guard by the skill of her acting and the "glamour" of her presence.

In this same month Parliament met for the first time since Mary's arrival in Scotland, and Knox confidently expected that the Treaty of Leith would be ratified, and the establishment of religion by the Parliament of 1560 would be put beyond all question by its action. But he was doomed to disappointment. The "holy water of the court" had not been without effect; the Protestant leaders had slackened in their enthusiasm, and what he regarded as a great opportunity was lost. He expostulated with many of the principal men of the party on the subject, but his efforts were in vain; and the "contention" between him and Murray over it was "so sharp" that there was a breach of friendship between them which lasted for more than a year. The effect of all this upon him was exceeding depressing; and on a Sunday before the dissolution of Parliament he took occasion to unburden his soul to his congregation. He expressed his sadness at the thought that those who had in their hands the opportunity to establish God's cause had actually betrayed it; he affirmed that the Parliament by which the Protestant Confession was adopted and the Church reformed was as free and lawful as any ever held in Scotland; and as reports of the Queen's marriage were now in circulation, he warned them of the consequences that would ensue if she should marry a papist. His words gave great offence to many Protestants as well as Romanists; and when the Queen heard of them {170} he was again summoned into her presence. This was the occasion on which the much talked of "tears" were so plentifully shed, and therefore we may reproduce the account of it given by McCrie, which is itself only a condensation into the language of to-day of the narrative given by Knox in his History.

"Her Majesty received him in a very different manner from what she had done at Loch Leven. Never had prince been handled (she passionately exclaimed) as she was: she had borne with him in all his rigorous speeches against herself and her uncles; she had offered unto him audience whenever he pleased to admonish her. 'And yet,' said she, 'I cannot be quit of you. I vow to God I shall be once revenged.' On pronouncing these words with great violence she burst into a flood of tears which interrupted her speech. When the Queen had composed herself, he proceeded calmly to make his defence. Her grace and he had (he said) at different times been engaged in controversy, and he never before perceived her offended with him. When it should please God to deliver her from the bondage of error in which she had been trained, through want of instruction in the truth, he trusted that her Majesty would not find the liberty of his tongue offensive. Out of the pulpit, he thought, few had occasion to be offended with him; but there he was not master of himself, but bound to obey Him who commanded him to speak plainly, and to flatter no flesh on the face of the earth.

"'But what have you do with my marriage?' said the {171} Queen. He was proceeding to state the extent of his commission as a preacher, and the reasons which led him to touch on that delicate subject; but she interrupted him by repeating her question: 'What have ye to do with my marriage? Or what are you in this commonwealth?' 'A subject born within the same, madame,' replied the Reformer, piqued by the last question, and the contemptuous tone in which it was proposed. 'And albeit I be neither earl, lord, nor baron in it, yet has God made me (how abject that ever I be in your eyes) a profitable member within the same. Yea, madame, to me it appertains no less to forewarn of such things as may hurt it, if I foresee them, than it doth to any of the nobility; for both my vocation and conscience requires plainness of me. And therefore, madame, to yourself I say that which I spake in public place: whensoever the nobility of this realm shall consent that ye be subject to an unfaithful husband, they do as much as in them lieth to renounce Christ, to banish His truth from them, to betray the freedom of this realm, and perchance shall in the end do small comfort to yourself.' At these words the Queen began again to weep and sob with great bitterness. The superintendent (Erskine of Dun, who was present), who was a man of mild and gentle spirit, tried to mitigate her grief and resentment: he praised her beauty and her accomplishments, and told her that there was not a prince in Europe who would not reckon himself happy in gaining her hand. During this scene, the severe and inflexible mind of the Reformer displayed {172} itself. He continued silent, and with unaltered countenance, until the Queen had given vent to her feelings. He then protested that he never took delight in the distress of any creature; it was with great difficulty that he could see his own boys weep when he corrected them for their faults, far less could he rejoice in her Majesty's tears; but seeing he had given her no just reason of offence, and had only discharged his duty, he was constrained, though unwillingly, to sustain her tears, rather than hurt his conscience and betray the commonwealth through his silence.

"This apology inflamed the Queen still more: she ordered him immediately to leave her presence, and wait the signification of her pleasure in the adjoining room. There he stood as 'one whom men had never seen'; all his friends (Lord Ochiltree excepted) being afraid to show him the smallest countenance. In this situation he addressed himself to the court ladies, who sat in their richest dress in the chamber. 'O fair ladies, how pleasing were this life of yours, if it should ever abide, and then, in the end, that we might pass to heaven with all this gay gear! But fie upon that knave Death, that will come whether we will or not!' Having engaged them in a conversation, he passed the time till Erskine came and informed him that he was allowed to go home until her Majesty had taken further advice. The Queen insisted to have the judgment of the Lords of Articles, whether the words he had used in the pulpit were not actionable; but she was persuaded to desist from a {173} prosecution. 'And so that storm quieted in appearance, but never in the heart.'"[1]

At this time, when many of his friends were cold toward him, an effort was made by some of his enemies to blacken his moral character by accusing him of a vile offence, but the lie had nothing in it to make it formidable. It was "a lie that was all a lie," and so it could be "met and fought with outright." The vindication was so complete that now very few remember that the allegation was ever made, and we refer to it here only to show that he too was made an illustration of the poet's words: "Be thou as chaste as ice, as pure as snow, thou shalt not escape calumny."

Much more serious was the attempt made about this same time to convict him of high treason. During the absence of Mary in Stirling, and on the day of the observance of the communion in the Protestant churches, her servants at Holyrood had taken measures for having the mass celebrated with more than usual publicity and splendour. The result was a scene of confusion and "brawling," almost indeed of riot, which was caused by the interference of some Protestants who were present. Two of these were afterwards indicted for their offence, which was called in the technical language of the country and the time, "forethought felony, hame-sucken, and invasion of the palace." Knox had been empowered by a general commission from the Church to ask the presence of the Protestant leaders in Edinburgh for {174} consultation and assistance in any emergency which in his judgment might require the same; and believing that the prosecution of these men might issue in very serious consequences, he drew up under the advice of the friends with whom he usually acted a circular letter, which he sent to the principal gentlemen of the "congregation," stating the circumstances, and asking them without fail to come to Edinburgh for the trial. A copy of this letter found its way into the hands of Mary, who laid it before the Privy Council, by whom it was pronounced to be treasonable. The Queen was exultant. Now was her opportunity, and she resolved to turn it to the best advantage. An extraordinary meeting of the councillors and other noblemen was convened to be held at Edinburgh about the middle of December, 1563, to try the cause. Some urged Knox to acknowledge that he had done wrong, and cast himself on the Queen's mercy, but that he absolutely refused to do, because he did not believe that he had committed an offence; and when Secretary Maitland and Murray called upon him, and somewhat ungenerously sought to get out of him the nature of the defence which he meant to set up, he very wisely put an end to the conversation with them, and resolved to keep his own counsel until he was actually called to vindicate his conduct.

When the day came, he stood forth as the champion of the liberty of assembly, as before he had appeared in vindication of free speech; and so admirably did he plead his cause that he was acquitted, if not unanimously {175} at least nem. con., of the charge which had been brought against him.

Much has been said of the bearing of Knox towards Queen Mary, and said, as we believe, most unjustly, for though he felt himself constrained to oppose her course, and would not yield to her wishes, yet he was never rude, or irreverent, or ungentlemanly. As Carlyle says, "he was never in the least ill-tempered with her Majesty;" and most of those who accuse him in this matter, we shrewdly suspect, have never read the accounts of his interviews with her, but have simply accepted the common babblement which has been so long current regarding them. No candid student of the rehearsal of these interviews in Knox's History, we are sure, could refuse to endorse the accuracy of Carlyle's statement of the case when he says "Mary often enough bursts into tears, oftener than once into passionate long continued fits of weeping, Knox standing with mild and pitying visage, but without the least hair's-breadth of recanting or recoiling, waiting till the fit pass, and then with all softness but with all inexorability taking up his theme again."

But while Knox's manner toward her Majesty has been most microscopically examined, very little attention has been given to Mary's manner toward Knox; and on this particular occasion, in the presence of the council and the nobles, sitting too as a kind of court before which he was on trial for high treason, it was flippant and unmannerly in the extreme, and was besides entirely {176} incompatible with the presence in her of a judicial spirit. When she entered the chamber and took her seat, she first smiled, and then burst into a loud guffaw, saying, "This is a good beginning, but wot you whereat I laugh? That man made me weep, and shed never a tear himself. I will see now if I can make him weep." Then after his letter had been read, and he was defending himself, she cried, "What is this? Methinks you trifle with him. Who gave him authority to make convocation of my lieges? Is not that treason?" There spake the despot, for beneath the velvet of her glove there was always a hand of iron; but she touched a chord that vibrated to a note which she had not thought to sound when she used these words, for Ruthven said boldly and categorically, "No, madame!" The gruff nobleman was immediately commanded by her Majesty to "hold his peace," and Knox went on with his defence in such a way that he successfully vindicated his right to call and hold a meeting of his friends for any lawful purpose when and where he chose. He was next questioned about the statement in his letter to the effect that he feared the prosecution of these men would open a door for the infliction of cruelty upon a greater number; and as he was proceeding to enlarge upon the deeds of the papists in France, and denouncing those who had done them, he was interrupted by the ejaculation of one of the nobles, "You forget yourself; you are not in the pulpit." This called forth the often quoted words, "I am in the place where I am demanded of my {177} conscience to speak the truth; and, therefore, the truth I speak; impugn it who so list." The Queen now felt that a defeat was imminent, and as a last resort, she tried to work on the sympathy of her lords by referring once more, but this time in another fashion, to the fact that Knox had made her weep. That, however, only gave him an opportunity of rehearsing all that had occurred on the occasion to which she had referred, and thereby made his victory the more sure. But what is to be said of her conduct throughout on this trial? "Heard you ever, my lords, a more despiteful and treasonable letter?" "You shall not escape so." "Is it not treason to accuse a prince of cruelty?" "Lo! what say you to all that?" These are a few of her expressions when she was sitting as a judge, and with these, and others already quoted, before us, is it not idle to speak of justice, far less of mannerliness or gentlewomanliness in the case? Ungentlemanliness is bad enough,--though even of that we maintain that there was nothing in Knox's treatment of his queen,--but to seek to overbear a court as Mary did at this time, by the manifestation of her eagerness to have the accused condemned, either by fair means or foul, is infinitely worse. The spirit of Mary here was that of Jeffreys long after. It was indeed far from being so coarsely and brutally expressed, but it is worthy of all reprobation, and in view of the facts which we have here presented, it is little wonder that Hume, in writing to the historian Robertson, should have said, "I am afraid that you, as well as myself, have drawn Mary's character {178} with too great softenings. She was undoubtedly a violent woman at all times." But he never altered his representation in his work, and to him, perhaps, more than to all others, the prevalent misconception of our Reformer's character, manner, and motives is to be traced.

The result of this trial was announced by Secretary Maitland, when he said to Knox that he was at liberty to return home for that night. But though his voice was smooth, his soul was full of wrath, and Mary's mortification vented itself in taunting the very man who had given her the letter, for voting for the acquittal of him who wrote it. Thus again the Reformer triumphed, and it is with a glow of satisfaction akin to that with which Nehemiah recounts his escape from Sanballat, that he finishes the record thus: "That night was neither dancing nor fiddling in the court, for madame was disappointed of her purpose, which was to have had John Knox in her will, by vote of her nobility."

CHAPTER XII.

MINISTRY AT EDINBURGH, 1564-1570.

In the month of March, 1564, Knox, who had been a widower for now rather more than three years, was united in marriage to Margaret Stewart, daughter of Lord Ochiltree, and the room in the old baronial residence where the ceremony was performed is still pointed out to visitors. Despite their dissimilarity in age, the union seems to have been a very happy one, and such as brightened the last days of the Reformer's home life. This year passed with little to make it memorable save a long discussion between Knox and Secretary Maitland, which originated in an attempt to restrain the freedom of the Reformer's utterances on public questions in the pulpit, and wandered over a great variety of topics, touching, among others, the duties of magistrates and their subjects, but led to no immediate practical result. The calm, however, was not of long continuance, for we come now to those troublous times and dark doings which have made the reign of Mary Queen of Scots the great debating ground of modern history. She determined to marry Lord {180} Henry Darnley, the son of the Earl of Lennox, a Catholic and an empty-headed fool. The knowledge of her purpose provoked the project of an insurrection among some of her nobles, who were headed by the Earl of Murray; but though they had the promise of assistance from Elizabeth, she failed them when it came to the point, and the result was that all who had been concerned in it were proclaimed as outlaws and banished from the kingdom. In this affair Knox took no part whatever, though Lord Ochiltree, his father-in-law, was implicated in it, and was one of the exiles. But though he did not compromise himself by proposing to join in the meditated appeal to arms, he was as strongly opposed to Mary's marriage as any of them, and as was his wont he liberated his conscience in the pulpit, but it was not until after the nuptials had been consummated that his words were especially regarded. The marriage was celebrated on the 29th of July, 1565, and on the 19th of August, Darnley, for some reason, chose to attend the public services in St. Giles' Cathedral, where a great throne had been prepared for his reception. Whether Knox had received any intimation of his intention to be present we are unable to say, but in his sermon there were two things which gave great offence to this prominent hearer. The first was his quotation of the passage, "I will give children to be their princes, and babes shall rule over them; children are their oppressors, and women rule over them"; and the second, his declaration that "God had punished Ahab because {181} he did not correct his idolatrous wife Jezebel." Darnley believed that these words were meant for him, and went home in the sulks, making his likeness to Ahab only the more striking by refusing to eat his dinner. The preacher was immediately summoned before the Privy Council, by whom he was told that he must desist from preaching as long as their majesties were in the city. For his own exoneration Knox printed the sermon for the preaching of which he was thus condemned, and it remains the only specimen of his pulpit work proper which has come down to us. It is founded on Isaiah xxvi. 13-21, and is of the nature of an expository discourse, bringing out the primary signification and reference of the words, and making application of the principles evolved by that process to the characters and circumstances of his hearers. It gives evidence of considerable scholarship, of immense familiarity with Scripture, of good acquaintance with ancient history, and of great fervour of spirit. It is neither a hasty nor ill digested production, and it impresses us a good deal more by its solidity than by its invective. Indeed, there are in it no passages that one could put into comparison for that with others which have been already mentioned by us; and it is a little difficult for the modern reader to wed in his imagination a style so calm and weighty as that which he finds here, with a manner so vehement as the Reformer's is usually described to have been. But no printer can reproduce the man, or the surroundings; here are the wood and the lamb indeed; but in these {182} others were the fire--from heaven too in a sense--which flamed forth with its energizing and consuming power, and made his discourse a thing of might. Such difference as there is between a bugle, and a bugle blown by a living martial musician, there is between a printed sermon and the same discourse preached by its author with the glow of spiritual enthusiasm in his heart and on his face. The one is a thing of curious study to the professional man, the other is a trumpet call which puts heart and heroism into hundreds in a moment.

Knox showed his law-abiding spirit by obeying the injunction of the authorities. His biographer, indeed, says that "it does not appear that he continued any time suspended from preaching," but Dr. Laing believes that he did not resume his usual ministrations at Edinburgh, unless at occasional intervals, until after Queen Mary had been deprived of her authority. He was not idle, however, in those months, for he was employed not only in the preparation of his "History of the Reformation in Scotland," but also in the visitation of churches in the south of Scotland, and in a journey into England, specially undertaken to look after his two boys whom he had sent thither for education.

In this interval occurred the murder of David Rizzio, on the 9th March, 1566, in the palace of Holyrood. That wretched man was an Italian adventurer, whose knowledge of foreign languages made him useful to Mary in her correspondence with the other members of the Anti-Protestant League to which she belonged. {183} His acquaintance with her political designs thence derived opened the way for his becoming one of the most confidential of her advisers. That roused against him the enmity of the Scottish nobles, and Darnley became jealous of his intimacy with the Queen; so with his assistance and approval David was foully slain almost before the eyes of his mistress. Attempts have been made to implicate Knox with this affair, but though he does not conceal his satisfaction at David's "removal," he was in no wise accessory to his death. The very next day after this tragedy the exiled lords returned to Edinburgh, and then followed thick and fast upon each other events of great and lasting importance to the land. These were the birth of James VI. on the 19th of June, 1566; the murder of Darnley, on the night between the 9th and 10th of February, 1567, a deed which was planned and carried out by Bothwell and his agents, not without dark grounds for the suspicion, to say the very least, that he and they were acting with the knowledge and consent of Mary herself; the marriage on the 15th May, 1567, of Mary to Bothwell, that black-hearted villain who was the evil genius of her life; the surrender of Mary to the opposing Lords at Carberry Hill on the 15th of June; the imprisonment of Mary in Loch Leven Castle, where, on the 24th of July, she signed a deed abdicating the crown in favour of her infant son, and appointing Murray regent during his minority; the escape of Mary from her place of confinement on the 2nd of May, 1568; and the defeat on May 13th of her {184} forces at Langside, whence she fled to seek from Elizabeth refuge in England, with the Fotheringay block as the ultimate result. For full details regarding all of these we must refer our readers to the Scottish histories, and we content ourselves with mentioning them thus in a group in order that we may carry in our hands the clue for the intelligent following out of our Reformer's career.

When the infant James was crowned in the parish church of Stirling, on the 29th of July, 1567, the sermon on the occasion was preached by Knox, though he objected to perform the ceremony of anointing, which accordingly was done by another. In the month of December following he preached at the opening of Parliament, and had the satisfaction of seeing an Act passed which ratified all that had been done in the way of Reformation by the Parliament of 1560; while an additional statute was now made providing that no prince should afterwards be admitted to exercise authority in the kingdom without taking an oath to maintain the Protestant religion.

During the regency of Murray everything went well, but his assassination (what terrible times these were!) at Linlithgow, by Hamilton of Bothwellhaugh, on the 23rd of January, 1569, was a terrible blow to Knox. Indeed, it may be said that he was never quite the same man afterwards. Knox and Murray loved and trusted each other thoroughly--perhaps all the more from the additional insight into each other's hearts {185} which their temporary estrangement gave them, and when the Regent was stricken down the Reformer felt as if his chief human helper had been taken from him. Murray was a genuine patriot, and in the main a sincere and noble man. He had his faults, and on exceptional occasions like that described by Froude,[1] when he was made the tool of Elizabeth, he was constrained to be, at least by his silence, a party to deceit which in his heart he abhorred; but that historian has not hesitated to call him "a noble gentleman of stainless honour,"[2] and to affirm that "his noble nature had no taint of self in it";[3] and though Robertson has done his best to belittle him, the verdict of history we think will settle in the acceptance of Spottiswood's eulogy: "a man truly good, and worthy to be ranked among the best governors that this kingdom hath enjoyed, and therefore to this day honoured with the title of 'the good Regent.'" On the Sunday after this irreparable loss, Knox poured out his heart to God before the congregation in a prayer which showed how deeply the bereavement had depressed his spirit, and on the day of the funeral he preached a sermon from the text, "Blessed are the dead that die in the Lord," in which he sketched the character and career of his friend with such effect that three thousand persons were moved to tears by his words. The blow fell sorely on the country; and it nearly crushed the {186} Reformer. The loss preyed upon his spirit and enfeebled his strength, so that in the month of October following he was stricken with paralysis or apoplexy, which laid him aside altogether for a season from his work, and gave warning of the approaching end. His enemies exulted over his illness, and could not refrain from congratulating themselves on the prospect that he would never preach again; but after some weeks he so far regained his vigour as to resume, in part at least, those labours in which he had found so much of his joy. Throughout the winter and the spring he continued to bear testimony from his pulpit to the principles which he had so long proclaimed, and to expose and rebuke the evil-doers who were once more at work in the land. For though the murder of Murray brought no permanent advantage to the party of reaction, it brought back again, for a while at least, the chaos and contentions out of which he had begun to bring order and peace. Lennox, as the grandfather of the infant king, was put into the place of Murray, but within a comparatively brief period he was mortally wounded in an assault made upon the adherents of the king at Stirling, by a force led by Huntly in the interests of Mary, and Erskine of Mar was chosen as his successor. This was in September, 1571. Meanwhile Kirkaldy, of Grange, who had been appointed governor of the Castle of Edinburgh by Murray, had turned his back upon the professions and promise of his life, by avowing himself a partisan of the Queen. He held that fortress for her {187} behoof, and gave its protection to Secretary Maitland, who was working earnestly in her cause. By Maitland's influence Kirkaldy was encouraged in a course which was exceedingly painful to Knox. The Laird of Grange and he had been fellow-sufferers in the French galleys, and to the last the heart of the Reformer yearned after him. Yet he could not permit his conduct as governor of the Castle to go unreproved. On two occasions, in particular, he was constrained to take public notice of his doings. The first was briefly this. There had been a scuffle in Dunfermline between a cousin of Kirkaldy and his relatives, and some of the Duries, a family with whom the Kirkaldys had a feud; and one of the latter having been seen shortly afterwards in the streets of Edinburgh, was by Kirkaldy's orders followed to Leith by some of his tools, that they might chastise him with a cudgel. But they took the sword instead and left him dead. In the attempt to escape, one of the assailants was arrested and committed to the Tolbooth, but Grange and his men attacked the building, violently forced it open, and marched off with their liberated comrade to the Castle, the guns of which they fired, either in token of triumph or for the purpose of striking terror into the citizens. In his sermon on the following Sunday Knox protested against this interference with the course of justice, using language which seems to us both temperate and kindly: "Had it been done," he said, "by the authority of a bloodthirsty man, or one who had no fear of God, he would not have been so much {188} moved; but he was affected to think that one, of whom all good men had formed so great expectations, should have fallen so low as to act such a part, one too who, when formerly in prison, had refused to purchase his own liberty by the shedding of blood." An utter misrepresentation of this statement was carried to Kirkaldy, who complained to John Craig, the Reformer's colleague, by whom he was referred to the elders of the Church of which Kirkaldy still professed to be a member. Knox himself, as soon as he had the matter brought before him, denied that he had used the words imputed to him, and took the first opportunity of correcting the false report, by repeating and vindicating what he had really said.

The other occasion was that of the appearance shortly after, in the church, of Kirkaldy, accompanied by a strong armed escort, composed of those who had been most conspicuous in the recent outrages. He had not attended the public services for nearly a year, and Knox looked upon his presence so surrounded as an attempt to overawe him. But he was not the man to be thus intimidated, and so, as his good servant Ballantyne tells us, he took occasion then and there to inveigh "against all such as forget God's benefits received, and in treating of God's great mercies bestowed upon penitents, according to his common manner, he forewarned proud contemners that

God's mercy appertained not to such as with knowledge proudly transgressed, and after, more proudly maintained the same." Kirkaldy was greatly {189} enraged at these words, and even in the church he gave vent to his anger so loudly as to be heard by a great part of the congregation. The report went out in consequence that he meant to kill the preacher; but Knox held on his way, dealing defiantly with the anonymous libels that were sent him, and publicly declaring in words that have become proverbial, that "from Isaiah, Jeremiah, and other inspired writers, he had learned to call a fig a fig, and a spade a spade."

But when, in 1571, Kirkaldy received the Hamiltons and their forces into the Castle, the friends of Knox became seriously alarmed for his safety. They proposed to form a guard who should constantly accompany him for his protection; but he would not accept the offer, and even if he had accepted it Kirkaldy would not have permitted it to be carried out. It was according to military etiquette that he should suppress or prevent all such outrages, and he expressed his willingness to provide a guard for Knox from the soldiers of his garrison. He even tried to get the Hamiltons to guarantee the safety of the Reformer, but they declared that they could not enter into any such engagement, "because there were many rascals and others among them who loved him not, who might do him harm without their knowledge." One evening a musket was fired into his window, and had he not been sitting in a place different from that which he usually occupied, the ball must have struck him, and would in all probability have mortally wounded him. After that he {190} was importuned by his friends to seek a place of safety elsewhere, but he refused to leave his post until they told him that they had made up their minds to defend him, if need be, with their lives, and that if blood was shed they would leave it on his head. This argument prevailed, and he consented to remove to St. Andrews, whither he went by easy stages, and where he arrived in the month of May, 1571. In his absence his pulpit in St. Giles was filled for a while by Alexander Gordon, Bishop of Galloway, who pleased the Queen's party but displeased the vast majority of the Protestants, so that the Church of Edinburgh was for a time dissolved, while disorder reigned in the city, and what was virtually a civil war was raging in the country.

CHAPTER XIII.

LAST DAYS, 1570-1572.

At St. Andrews Knox was free from personal danger, and resumed the work of preaching. In the pulpit of the parish church he discoursed almost regularly, with a vigour which triumphed for the time over his physical weakness. We have a most graphic portrait of him at this time from the pen of James Melville who was then a student at the University, and who writes thus in his diary: (We are constrained to modernize the words that they may be generally understood by English and American readers, but we know how much they must lose thereby in expressiveness, to those who understand the vernacular) "Of all the benefits that I had that year (1571), was the coming of that most notable prophet and apostle of our nation, Mr. John Knox, to St. Andrews, who by the faction of the Queen occupying the castle and town of Edinburgh, was compelled to remove therefrom, with a number of the best, and chose to come to St. Andrews. I heard him teach there the prophecies of Daniel that summer and the winter following. I had my pen and my little {192} book, and took away such things as I could comprehend. In the opening up of his text he was moderate for the space of half an hour; but when he entered on application, he made me so to shudder (scottice, 'grue') and tremble, that I could not hold my pen to write. He was very weak. I saw him every day of his teaching, go slowly and warily, with a fur of martens about his neck, a staff in the one hand, and good, godly Richard Ballantyne, his servant, holding up the other armpit (scottice, 'oxter'), from the abbey to the parish kirk, and by the said Robert and another servant lifted up to the pulpit, where he behoved to lean at his first entrance; but before he had done with his sermon, he was so active and vigorous, that it seemed as if he would beat the pulpit in pieces (scottice, 'ding the pulpit in blads') and fly out of it." Nor must we omit this other trait, evincing as it does the interest taken by the aged warrior in the young soldiers who were then just girding on their armour. "He would sometimes come in and rest in our college yard, and call us scholars unto him, and bless us, and exhort us to know God, and His work in our country, and stand by the good cause, to use our time well, and learn the good instructions and follow the good example of our masters."

In St. Andrews too, at this time, he published his "Answer to the Letter of a Jesuit named Tyrie," which was the last work that he gave to the world. It had been composed years before, in the haste which was incident to his numerous occupations, but it was now {193} revised and enlarged, and gives expression in a vigorous manner to his maturest views on faith, religion, and the Catholic, or true and Universal Church. Here is a nugget from it, not without its pertinence to some popular notions current in the days in which we live. "We find that Christ sends not His afflicted Church to seek a lineal succession of any persons, before He will receive them; but He with all gentleness calleth His sheep unto Himself, saying, 'Come unto Me all ye that labour and are laden, and I will ease you.'" Truly a golden sentence, touching the very quick of all Church controversies, and emphasizing the principle never to be forgotten, that we must find our way to the Church through Christ, and not to Christ through the Church.

In public questions he did not cease to take an interest, although the state of his health unfitted him for active leadership. Still, that he was no unconcerned spectator of what was going forward is apparent from the following statement, which, because of its faithfulness and fairness, we take from the article by Dr. Mitchell on "The Last Days of John Knox."[1] "In March, 1572, the General Assembly was held in St. Andrews, in the schools of St. Leonard's College. This place was no doubt chosen, in part at least, for the convenience of the aged Reformer, whose counsel in that time of trouble was specially needed. It was the last Assembly at which he was able to be present, and probably the first witnessed by Davidson and Melville. 'There,' the {194} latter narrates, 'was motioned the making of bishops, to the which Mr. Knox opposed himself directly and zealously.' ... Some months before this a convention at Leith had given its sanction to a sort of mongrel episcopacy, nominally to secure the tithes more completely to the Church, but really to secure the bulk of them by a more regular title to certain covetous noblemen, who sought in this way to reimburse themselves for their services in the cause." (The noblemen presented to the bishoprics men who had first covenanted to give by far the larger portion of the revenues to the patrons, and with a truly Scottish humour, the people called these dignitaries "tulchan bishops," a "tulchan" being the name which was given to a calf's skin stuffed with straw, which was set up to make the cow give her milk more willingly.) "First among these noblemen was the Earl of Morton, then one of the chief supporters of the young prince, and soon after Regent of the kingdom. Having secured a presentation to the Archbishopric of St. Andrews, for Mr. John Douglas, he came over to the city, had him elected in terms of the convention, and on the 10th of February inaugurated into his office. This was performed by Winram, superintendent of Fife, according to the order followed in the admission of superintendents, save that the Bishops of

Caithness, the Superintendent of Lothian, and Mr. David Lindsay, who sat beside Douglas, laid their hands on his head. Knox had preached that day as usual, but, as Ballantyne is careful to tell us, "had {195} refused to inaugurate the said bishop"; and, as others add, had denounced "anathema to the giver, and anathema to the receiver," who, as rector and principal, "had already far more to do than such an aged man could hope to overtake." In the face of such a fact, it is idle for historians to insinuate, as Burton does, that Knox gave in his closing days even a quasi sanction to episcopacy.

In the month of July, 1572, a cessation of hostilities for a time was agreed upon between the Regent's party and that of the Queen, so that the city of Edinburgh was again delivered from annoyance, either at the hands of the garrison or of "the lewd fellows of the baser sort" who made its streets unsafe. As Melville says, "the good and honest men thereof returned to their homes, and earnestly implored their pastor, if he could without injury of his health, to do the same; and so Mr. Knox and his family passed home to Edinburgh," where he arrived on the 23rd of August. On the following Sunday he preached in his old pulpit; but as in his weakness he could not make himself heard in the large cathedral, the western part of the nave, known as the Tolbooth Church, was fitted up for his use; and that was the scene of his latest ministrations. He preached as often as he was able, delivering a course of sermons on the Redeemer's Passion, which he had always wished to be the theme of his last discourses. But in his debilitated condition, his ancient power had well-nigh departed. Only once during this period of decadence {196} did the "wonted fires" flame forth out of "their ashes." When he heard of the massacre of St. Bartholomew he had himself assisted into the pulpit, and there, moved at once by the tender recollections of the many friends of his own who had been among the victims, and by his life-long antagonism to the system which was identified with that horrible cruelty, he thundered forth the vengeance of Heaven against "that cruel murderer the king of France;" and turning to Le Croc, the French ambassador, he said, like another Elijah: "Go tell your master that sentence is pronounced against him; that the Divine vengeance shall never depart from him or from his house, except they repent; but his name shall remain an execration to posterity, and none proceeding from his loins shall enjoy his kingdom in peace."

His closing work was the installation of his own successor. During his absence from Edinburgh, Mr. John Craig, his colleague, had gone to another sphere of labour, and his flock had now no other shepherd than himself. He was, therefore, very naturally anxious to see some true and earnest man set over them in the Lord, and accordingly obtained permission from the General Assembly to induct any minister who might be chosen by himself, the Superintendent of Lothian, and the Church of Edinburgh, to take his place. They agreed to nominate James Lawson, of Aberdeen, who, being urged by Knox to repair immediately to Edinburgh, in a touching letter, with a still more touching postscript,--"Haste, lest ye come too late!"--came to {197} the metropolis, gave such evidence of his gifts as satisfied all parties concerned, and was installed on the 9th of November. Knox preached the sermon on the occasion in the Tolbooth Church, and after that removed with the congregation to the larger area of the cathedral, where he went through the form of admission by proposing the usual questions, and giving exhortation first to the pastor and then to the people. He concluded with prayer and the benediction; "then leaning upon his staff and the arm of an attendant, he crept down the street, which was lined with the audience, who, as if anxious to take the last sight of their beloved pastor, followed him until he entered his house, from which he never again came out alive."

The next day he was seized with a violent cough, and he gradually declined until the 24th of November, when, at the age of sixty-seven, he breathed his last. His faithful servant, Richard Ballantyne, has left a minute description of his death-bed experiences and sayings, which Dr. McCrie has reproduced the main features of in his biography. We select those which seem to us to give most insight into the character of the man. Visited, a few days after his last sickness began, by two of his personal friends, he "for their cause came to the table," for it was the hour of dinner, and caused an hogshead of wine in the cellar to be pierced for their entertainment, at the same time playfully desiring one of them to send for some of it as long as it lasted, for he would not tarry until it was all drunk." To the elders of his Church who {198} came in a body to his room at his request, he said, "I profess before God and His holy angels that I never made merchandise of the sacred word of God; never studied to please men; never indulged my own private passions or those of others, but faithfully distributed the talents entrusted to me for the edification of the Church over which I watched. Whatever obloquy wicked men may cast upon me respecting this point, I rejoice in the testimony of a good conscience." As they were leaving, he detained his colleague and the minister of Leith to give them a message to Kirkaldy of Grange, adding to it these words: "That man's soul is dear to me, and I would not have it perish, if I could save it." When they returned and told him that they had met with a rude reception, he was much grieved, and said, "that he had been earnest in prayer for that man, and still trusted that his soul would be saved, although his body should come to a miserable end." Such petitions as these dropped from his lips at intervals, "Come, Lord Jesus. Be merciful to Thy Church which Thou hast redeemed. Give peace to this afflicted commonwealth. Raise up faithful pastors who will take the charge of Thy Church. Grant us, Lord, the perfect hatred of sin, both by the evidences of Thy wrath and mercy." To his friend Fairley, of Braid, he said: "Every one bids me good-night, but when will you do it? I have been greatly indebted to you, for which I shall never be able to recompense you, but I commit you to one who can, to the eternal God." To Campbell of Kingzeancleugh {199} he said, "I must leave the care of my wife and children to you, to whom you must be a husband in my room." A few hours before his death he said to his wife, "Go read where I first cast my anchor," and she understanding his reference, read to him the 17th chapter of John's Gospel, and afterwards a part of Calvin's "Sermons on the Ephesians." Shortly after, seeing that death was fast approaching, and when he was unable to speak, his servant said to him, "Now, sir, the time that you have long called to God for, the end of your battle, is come; and seeing all natural power now fails you, remember the comfortable promises of our Saviour Jesus Christ, which ofttimes you have shown us. And that we may understand and know that you hear us, give us some sign." And "so he lifted up one of his hands, and incontinent thereafter rendered up his spirit, apparently without pain or movement, so that he seemed rather to fall asleep than to die."

He was buried on the 26th of November, his body being accompanied to the grave by a large concourse of people, among whom were the Earl of Morton, newly-appointed Regent, and other noblemen. According to the rubric of his own Book of Common Order, there was no religious service at the funeral, but when the body was lowered to its place Calderwood tells us that the Regent Morton uttered these words: "HERE LIETH A MAN WHO IN HIS LIFE NEVER FEARED THE FACE OF MAN; WHO HATH BEEN OFTEN THREATENED WITH DAGGE AND DAGGER, BUT YET HATH ENDED HIS DAYS IN PEACE {200} AND HONOUR." The precise site of his grave cannot now be identified. It was in the churchyard of St. Giles, which extended from the church down the slope of the hill till it reached the Colgate, and was wholly obliterated in 1633 when the Parliament House and other buildings were erected. If any stone ever marked the spot, it was probably then removed or destroyed. Tradition points out as the place that which is now marked with the letters "I.K., 1572," a few feet to the west of the statue of Charles II. in the Parliament Square. What Charles ever did for Scotland to deserve any such memorial, it would puzzle the wisest man to say, unless perhaps on the principle that it was his intolerance which most of all provoked the Revolution; but many will agree with Dr. Laing in thinking, that "a more appropriate monument for such a locality would be a statue of the great Reformer."

Knox, we are told, was of small stature, and his constitution never recovered from the effects of the exposure to which he was subjected in the French galleys, so that his frame was not well fitted for hardship and fatigue. He too had his "thorn in the flesh," and that he did so much in spite of that is a proof of the dominating power of his spiritual earnestness over his physical weakness. Of the five portraits reproduced and criticised so characteristically by Carlyle in his "Brochure" on the subject, we give our verdict in favour of that which he calls the Somerville portrait, and of which he says that it is "the only probable likeness anywhere known to {201} exist." It is that of a true Scottish face--sharp, wedge-like in its contour, surmounted by a bald dome-like head fringed with scanty hair, the beard short and not very profuse, the lips firmly set, with the slightest curl of scorn in their expression, and the eyes small, clear, penetrating, and quick; altogether "a physiognomy worth looking at," and far more in keeping with the character and history of the Reformer, than the long-bearded timber-looking figure-head, surmounted by a Genevan cap, which has been made so long to represent him to posterity, and which Carlyle has shown to have no claim to authenticity.

His children were five in number. His two sons by his first wife became students in St. John's College, Cambridge, where Nathanael, the elder, died in 1580. Eleazar, the younger, after finishing his studies, became Vicar of Clacton Magna, and died in 1591. He too was buried at Cambridge; and, by the death of both, the family of the Reformer in the male line became extinct. His three daughters by his second wife were Martha, Margaret, and Elizabeth. Martha became the wife of Alexander Fairley, eldest son of Robert Fairley, of Braid, whom we have just seen at the Reformer's death-bed. Margaret married Zachary Pont, one of the Lords of Session, and latterly minister of St. Cuthbert's, Edinburgh. Elizabeth wedded John Welsh, best known as Minister of Ayr, who was banished for the part which he took in the holding of the General Assembly at Aberdeen in July, 1605, and spent many years as pastor of a {202} Protestant Church in France. It is of this daughter that the well-known story is told to the effect that when her husband's health failed she came over to London, and, having through the influence of friends obtained audience of King James I., requested the royal permission for his return to his native land. After some coarse pleasantry, which need not here be repeated, the king told her that if she would persuade her husband to submit to the bishops he would allow him to go back to Scotland, whereupon, lifting her apron and holding it out toward the king, she answered, like a true daughter of her father, "Please your Majesty, I'd rather kep his head (i.e. receive it from the block) there!"

Of the writings of Knox we have spoken incidentally in the course of our narrative, and need not therefore enter now into any minute criticism of their character and merits. They were struck out of him almost extemporaneously by emergencies that arose, and, like all similar productions, they were mainly ephemeral in their nature, so that they are studied now, for the most part, only by those who wish to gain some insight into the man, his times, and his work. He was not what might properly be called literary. He would not have described himself as another of his countrymen did, as "a writer of books." On the contrary, in the preface to the only sermon which he published, he affirmed that "he considered himself rather called of {203} God to instruct the ignorant, comfort the sorrowful, confirm the weak, and rebuke the proud by tongue and living voice in these most corrupt times, than to compose books for the age to come; seeing that so much is written (and that by men of most singular condition) and yet so little well observed, he decreed to contain himself within the bounds of that vocation whereunto he felt himself specially called." An exception to this may perhaps be found in his "History of the Reformation in Scotland," to which throughout we have been so much indebted, and which is one of the raciest, clearest, and most trustworthy records of the heroic struggle in which he was virtually the leader of the victorious side. It has been stigmatized by Burton as egotistical; but Carlyle more justly notices how on one occasion, when his personal merit far excelled all possible description, "he hardly names himself at all"; and where he could not be truthful without speaking of himself, he invariably does so in the third person, and without any attempt to glorify the work of which he might have said, "cujus pars magna fui." For the rest, as Carlyle says, "His account of every event he was present in is that of a well-discerning eye-witness. Things he did not himself see, but had reasonable cause and abundant means to inquire into--battles even, and sieges--are described with something of a Homeric vigour and simplicity." It is unfortunate for modern readers that it is written in the old Scottish dialect; but if some competent scholar would only honestly modernize and faithfully edit it, a {204} great boon would be conferred upon the present generation, for it has in it many elements of popular interest.

His special vocation was that of the preacher rather than of the author. The pulpit was the throne of his peculiar and pre-eminent power. Other men might equal or surpass him elsewhere, but there he was supreme. Different excellences might come out in himself on different occasions; but in the pulpit all his abilities were conspicuous, and there they were always at their best. It was the glass which focussed all his powers into a point, and quickened their exercise into a burning intensity which kindled everything it touched. It brightened his intellect, enlivened his imagination, clarified his judgment, inflamed his courage, and gave fiery energy to his utterance. He was never elsewhere so great in any one of these particulars, as he was, when in the pulpit, in them all; for there, over and above the "pr鎓 ervidum ingenium" which he had in common with so many of his countrymen, and the glow of animation which fills the soul of the orator when he looks upon an audience, he had the feeling that he was called of God to be faithful, and that made him almost like another Paul. Behind him was the cross of his Lord; before him was the throne at which he was to be accountable, and between these two he stood "watching for souls as one that must give account." He began his discourse most commonly with Biblical exposition, and spent a little time in calmly, clearly, and fully explaining the meaning of the passage on which he was engaged. In this {205} portion of his sermon, if we may judge from the published tracts which were apparently founded on pulpit utterances, he was clear, simple, convincing; not making a parade of learning, yet bringing out withal the true significance of the sacred text. Then having cleared away all doubt from that, he made it the foundation of a battery, whereon he erected a swivel gun, and with that he swept the whole horizon, firing at every evil which came within his view. Nor were the shots mere random things. They were deliberately aimed, and they commonly did most effective work. No matter who might be the evil-doer, the exposure was sure to be made, and the expostulation, usually ending in denunciation, unless the sinner should repent, was sure to follow. Whatever he might do elsewhere, he could neither shut his eyes nor keep back his utterance when he was, as he called it, "in public place." He was "set as a watchman" to the people of Scotland, and he would watch with wakeful vigilance, and give honest warning of everything which he saw wrong; for the wrong with him was always fraught with danger, and the wrongness was enough to evoke his protest. He used no soft words. He was no maker of polite phrases. He spoke in order to be understood, and therefore he "called a fig a fig, and a spade a spade." He went into the pulpit not because he had to say something, but because there was something in him which was compelling itself to be said. He spoke because he "could not but" speak. That irrepressibility gave {206} volcanic energy to his manner and fiery force to his words, so that the effects produced by his sermons were not merely superficial. Like those modern missiles which burst in the wounds which they have made, his words exploded within the hearts of those who had received them, and set them on fire with convictions that flamed forth in their conduct. It was apparently impossible for any one to listen to him without being deeply moved, either to antagonism, or to enthusiastic agreement, or--for he could be tender also--to tears.

It may be said indeed that he allowed himself too great liberty in commenting on public men and national affairs; and we may readily admit that in ordinary times, and especially in our altered circumstances, it would be unwise in most preachers to use the pulpit precisely as he did. But we have to bear in mind that the crisis through which his country was passing at the time, was as much religious as political, and that the pulpit was the only organ at his command. To his credit be it recorded, that he was, if not the first, at least one of the very first to perceive the importance of making and guiding public opinion aright. He saw that the people were to be the virtual rulers in the coming time; nay, he recognised in them the ultimate arbiters for the decision of the great matters which were then in debate, and therefore he would not take time to go to royal closets or noblemen's studies, but made his appeal to the people as a body, and the pulpit was the only place in which he could do that. The daily press was not then born; the {207} public meeting had not yet come into vogue; but what is now done by our editors in their columns, and by our statesmen in Midlothian campaigns, and such like, he did by his five weekly sermons in Edinburgh, and by his various preaching journeys in the south and west and north divisions of the kingdom.

He informed and aroused public opinion. He appealed to the people, speaking to them as one under oath to the King of kings the while; and when we put the matter in that light, we have at once the defence of his procedure and the explanation of his success.

He was not always wise; neither was he always discriminating in his utterances. Who is? who especially when surrounded by the difficulties with which he had to contend? and we may well forgive him his occasional indiscretions, when we think of the work which, in spite of these, he was honoured to accomplish. By that work he has earned the gratitude of posterity, and deserved a place among the men who are most worthy to be remembered in these times. By that work the entire face and future of Scotland were changed. She has made great progress in many directions since his day, and outgrown many of the limitations within which he would have restricted her; but the success of his work made it possible for her to become what she is to-day. The liberty, the literature, the philosophy, as well as the religion of Scotland, could not have developed into what they became without the Reformation; and without Knox, humanly speaking, the Reformation would not {208} have been at all, or at least would not have been what it actually became. He had not the lyric thrill of genius that vibrates in the songs of Robert Burns; but in his own way and to his own tune he sang, "A man's a man for a' that," two hundred years before the Ayrshire bard was born. He laid the foundation of that national popular education which has made Scotland at home so intelligent, and carried Scotsmen with honour abroad into all the countries under heaven; and though he would have protested very vehemently against the scepticism of Hume and others, yet the men who have made the Scottish school of philosophy illustrious, received, consciously or unconsciously, much of their impulse from his work. Add to this, that wherever Presbyterianism has found a foothold, its votaries name Knox side by side with Calvin, as one of its foremost leaders and organizers. But when we consider the shortness of the time within which Knox did his work for Scotland, the greatness of the man becomes still more conspicuous. He was forty-two years of age when he was called to preach in the Castle of St. Andrews, and he died at sixty-seven. Within these twenty-five years therefore his reformation work was done; and yet of these nearly two were spent as a galley-slave in French captivity, five were passed in England, three on the continent, and for the last year and a half of his life he was disabled by paralysis, so that his active labours in his native land were virtually condensed within little more than fourteen years. During these, also, he had to contend, save in the brief season {209} of Murray's regency, with the greatest difficulties, but through them all he held on, and over them all he secured an ultimate triumph. His energy was consuming, his zeal untiring, and his vigilance unslumbering. With the eye of a statesman he looked into the future, while at the same time he keenly scrutinized the movements of the present. He had the near sight which sees what is closest to it with admirable distinctness, and the far sight which descries with equal accuracy what is distant, and with these he combined the philosophic spirit which marked very correctly the connection between the two. He was a true patriot, and ever willing to sacrifice himself in the welfare of his country. And all these qualities in him were raised to the white heat of enthusiasm, and fused into the unity of holiness by his devotion to the God and Father of his Saviour the Lord Jesus Christ. He spoke, and wrote, and acted as ever in His sight. This was the secret of his courage, the root of his inflexibility, and the source of his power. As a Reformer he had in him the boldness of Luther, combined with some of the qualities of Calvin, and though as a whole he was inferior to both, yet more than either he reminds us of a Hebrew prophet. When we see him before Queen Mary, we think at once of Elijah before Ahab, and more appropriately perhaps than any other man in modern history he might have taken for the motto of his life the oft-repeated asseveration of the Tishbite, "As the Lord God of Israel liveth, before whom I stand."

{210}

And yet, though sternly uttering in the highest places what he believed to be the word of God, there were not wanting in his character other traits of gentleness and geniality. As Carlyle has truly said, "Tumult was not his element, it was the tragic feature of his life that he was forced to dwell in that." He too, like the granite mountains of his native land, had in him fountains of tenderness, and valleys laughing with cheerfulness. He was not the heartless Stoic that many have ignorantly painted him, for have we not seen him weeping with those who were "sobbing unto God"? And though it may seem strange to those who have not made themselves acquainted with his history, there was in him a vein of humour, yea even, as Carlyle says, of "drollery," that makes him excellent company. This humour of his, as the writer just named has admirably diagnosed it, was "not mockery, scorn, bitterness, alone, though there is enough of that too, but a true, loving, illuminating laugh mounts up over the earnest visage; not a loud laugh; you would say a laugh in the eyes most of all."

But now our task is done. We have tried to show honestly the man as he was, and to describe dispassionately the work which he did. He is, if not pre-eminently the Scotchman of history,--though we think a good claim might be established for him as such,--yet certainly one of "the three mightiest," or of "the first three" of his nation; and like the vine whose branches spread over the wall, his influence has gone in blessing to other lands, for in his work we have the root of the English {211} Revolution, and some of the seeds that were carried westward in the Mayflower, and sown in New England fields, had fallen from his hands. It is not inappropriate therefore that one whose labours in the ministry of the gospel have closely connected him alike with Scotland, England, and America, should pay this willing tribute to his name and work.

CPSIA information can be obtained
at www.ICGtesting.com
Printed in the USA
BVHW041557250422
635283BV00009B/1063